W9-CPM-225

Industrial Revolution Biographies

Industrial Revolution Biographies

James L. Outman
Elisabeth M. Outman
Matthew May, Editor

Detroit • New York • San Diego • San Francisco • Cleveland • New Haven, Conn. • Waterville, Maine • London • Munich

Industrial Revolution: Biographies

James L. Outman and Elisabeth M. Outman

Project Editor
Matthew May

Editorial
Allison McNeill, Diane Sawinski

Permissions
Margaret Chamberlain

Imaging and Multimedia
Robert Duncan, Lezlie Light

Product Design
Pamela A. E. Galbreath, Michelle DiMercurio

Composition
Evi Seoud

Manufacturing
Rita Wimberley

For more information, contact:
The Gale Group, Inc.
27500 Drake Rd.
Farmington Hills, MI 48331-3535
Or you can visit our Internet site at http://www.gale.com

Cover photograph of Ida Tarbell reproduced courtesy of the Library of Congress; cover photograph of John D. Rockefeller reproduced by permission of Getty Images; cover photograph of Samuel F. B. Morse reproduced courtesy of the Library of Congress; back cover photograph of Henry Ford reproduced by permission of the American Automobile Manufacturers Association.

LIBRARY OF CONGRESS CATALOGING-IN-PUBLICATION DATA

Outman, James L., 1946–

Industrial Revolution. Biographies / James L. Outman and Elisabeth M. Outman.

v. cm.

Includes bibliographical references and index.

ISBN 0-7876-6514-2 (hardcover : alk. paper)

1. Industrialists—Biography—Juvenile literature. 2. Industrial revolution—Juvenile literature. 3. Capitalists and financiers—Biography—Juvenile literature. 4. Inventors—Biography—Juvenile literature. [1. Industrialists. 2. Industrial revolution. 3. Capitalists and financiers. 4. Inventors.] I. Outman, Elisabeth M., 1951– II. Title.

HC29 .O98 200
330.9'034'0922–dc21

2002155421

Printed in the United States of America
10 9 8 7 6 5 4 3 2 1

Contents

Reader's Guide

The Industrial Revolution, which began in England in the middle of the eighteenth century and spread across the globe by the beginning of World War II, shaped a new world. The introduction of new technology into manufacturing processes at the heart of the revolution turned simple agricultural societies into complex industrial ones. Consequently, the way we worked, where we lived, and how we communicated with one another were altered. Governments, even the physical environment of the planet, were forever changed. The Industrial Revolution was in every sense a revolution.

Industrial Revolution: Biographies profiles twenty-five of the most dynamic figures of the Industrial Revolution, including economic philosophers Adam Smith and Karl Marx; financial barons James J. Hill and J. P. Morgan; innovators Henry Bessemer, Henry Ford, Robert Fulton, and Eli Whitney; crusading journalists Upton Sinclair and Ida Tarbell; and many others.

Informative sidebar boxes and more than fifty photographs augment the text. Each entry concludes with a list of further readings. Also included in the volume are a timeline of important events of the Industrial Revolution and a compre-

hensive index that allows easy access to the people, places, and subjects discussed throughout *Industrial Revolution: Biographies.*

Related reference sources

Industrial Revolution: Almanac, in eight chapters, provides an overview of this era, from its roots in the philosophies of the Renaissance to the first technological advances, from the first migrations of workers to urban areas to the rise of giant corporations. The volume includes nearly sixty photographs, sources for further study, a timeline, a glossary, and an index.

Industrial Revolution: Primary Sources presents twenty-seven full or excerpted written works, speeches, and testimony from the period. The volume includes excerpts from *An Inquiry into the Nature and Causes of the Wealth of Nations* by Adam Smith, *The Communist Manifesto* of Karl Marx, *Twenty Years at Hull-House* by Jane Addams, and the United States Supreme Court decision in *Northern Securities Co.* v. *United States* enforcing federal regulation of corporations. Each entry includes an introduction, things to remember while reading the excerpt, a glossary of difficult terms from the document, information on what happened after the work was published, and other interesting facts. Forty photographs, sources for further reading, a timeline, and an index supplement the volume.

Acknowledgments

The authors extend their thanks to U•X•L senior editor Diane Sawinski, U•X•L editor Matthew May, and U•X•L publisher Tom Romig for their assistance throughout the production of this series. Thanks, too, to U•X•L senior editor Allison McNeill for lending her editorial talents in the form of proofreading. The editor wishes to thank Marco Di Vita of the Graphix Group for always working with flexibility, speed, and, above all, quality.

Comments and suggestions

We welcome your comments on *Industrial Revolution: Biographies* and suggestions for other topics in history to consider. Please write: Editors, *Industrial Revolution: Biographies,* U•X•L, 27500 Drake Road, Farmington Hills, Michigan, 48331-3535; call toll-free: 800-877-4253; fax to 248-699-8097; or send e-mail via www.gale.com.

Industrial Revolution Timeline

1776 *An Inquiry into the Nature and Causes of the Wealth of Nations* by Scottish economist **Adam Smith** is published.

1781 Scottish engineer **James Watt** invents a rotary motion device for his steam engine.

1793 American inventor **Eli Whitney** develops and introduces the cotton gin.

June 14, 1798 Eli Whitney signs a contract with the U.S. government to produce 10,000 muskets in 28 months.

August 17, 1807 American engineer **Robert Fulton** launches his steamship *Clermont.* Two years later he obtains a patent from the U.S. government for his steamship.

1824 British industrialist **Robert Owen** purchases the town of New Harmony, Indiana, and attempts to implement his cooperative business ideas in an entire community.

September 27, 1825 **George Stephenson** operates his locomotive *Locomotion* along a 20-mile rail in England, the first time a steam locomotive hauls cars on a public railway.

1834 American inventor **Cyrus McCormick** takes out a patent on the first mechanical reaper.

May 1, 1844 American inventor **Samuel F. B. Morse** sends the first telegraph message from city to city, from Washington, D.C., to Baltimore, Maryland. Five years later he is granted a U.S. patent for the telegraph.

1848 *The Communist Manifesto,* written by German philosopher **Karl Marx** and his friend Frederich Engels, is published.

1856 British industrialist **Henry Bessemer** establishes the Bessemer process, in which steel could be made in more quantities for less money.

1864 Karl Marx organizes the International Workingmen's Association, also referred to as the First International.

1865 American businessman **John D. Rockefeller** purchases his first oil refinery.

1869 American financier **Jay Gould** begins his complex scheme of buying gold to lower the price of wheat that would be shipped on the railroads he owned.

1869 American inventor **George Westinghouse** takes a patent out on his invention of air brakes and forms Westinghouse Air Brake Company.

May 10, 1869 A golden spike is driven into the railroad tracks at Promontory, Utah, completing the first rail line to cross the United States.

1870 John D. Rockefeller and associates organize Standard Oil Company.

1873 With three partners, Canadian-American financier **James J. Hill** purchases the St. Paul & Pacific Railroad.

1881 British-American labor leader **Samuel Gompers** helps establish the Federation of Organized Trades and Labor Unions of the United States and Canada.

1881 Jay Gould buys Western Union to enhance his control of communication along railroad lines.

1889 John D. Rockefeller contributes $600,000 toward the founding of the University of Chicago, a project of the American Baptist Education Society.

1890 Irish-American labor leader Mary Harris Jones, better known as Mother Jones, is hired as a paid organizer by the United Mine Workers.

1890 *How the Other Half Lives,* by Danish-American journalist **Jacob Riis,** is published.

1892 Steel workers at American industrialist **Andrew Carnegie**'s Homestead Mill plant go on strike.

1899 Croatian-American inventor and scientist **Nikola Tesla** establishes a research laboratory in Colorado Springs, Colorado, to conduct his experiments with high voltage.

1901 American financier **J. P. Morgan** purchases Carnegie Company, Limited, the nation's leading steel company, for $480 million.

September 14, 1901 Following the death of William McKinley, **Theodore Roosevelt** becomes president of the United States.

February 18, 1902 The Theodore Roosevelt administration files a lawsuit against Northern Securities Co., claiming it is in violation of the Sherman Antitrust Act.

April 1903 The United States Supreme Court rules that the Northern Securities Company is an illegal trust (monopoly) and orders the company broken apart.

1904 *The Shame of the Cities,* by American journalist **Lincoln Steffens,** becomes a best-selling book in the United States.

1904 **Ida Tarbell**'s collection of articles on John D. Rockefeller is published as a book entitled *The History of the Standard Oil Company.*

1905 George Westinghouse converts the New York subway and elevated train systems to electric power.

1906 American journalist **Upton Sinclair**'s *The Jungle* is published.

October 1908 American engineer and industrialist **Henry Ford** introduces the Model T.

1912 American financier George Jay Gould, the son of Jay Gould, begins losing ownership control of many of his railroad lines. Seven years later, a court orders Gould to be removed as the executor and trustee of his father's estate.

1913 Mother Jones begins to lead strikes against John D. Rockefeller's coal mines in Colorado.

1919 A court orders George Jay Gould to be removed as the executor and trustee of his father's estate.

1919 Henry Ford resigns as president of the Ford Motor Company.

Industrial Revolution Biographies

Henry Bessemer

Born January 19, 1813
Charlton, England

Died March 15, 1898
London, England

British engineer, inventor

Henry Bessemer devised a quicker, more efficient way of making steel, which led to steel replacing cast iron as the metal of preference in making railroad tracks, military weapons, and structures like bridges and skyscrapers. His invention, the Bessemer furnace, or converter, enormously raised the annual production of steel in England and helped move along the Industrial Revolution, a period of fast-paced economic change that began in Great Britain in the middle of the eighteenth century. One of the first to adopt Bessemer's steelmaking process wholeheartedly was American industrialist **Andrew Carnegie** (1835–1919; see entry), who built a world-class fortune as a result.

"I had an immense advantage over many others dealing with the problem of reducing the cost of making steel inasmuch as I had no fixed ideas derived from long-established practice to control and bias my mind, and did not suffer from the general belief that whatever is, is right."

Bessemer is best known for his improved method of making steel, but he was a prolific inventor in other areas as well. For example, he developed a way to turn powdery graphite into lead pencils, and he invented a method of producing glittering gold-colored paint made from powdered bronze. He also invented a machine to turn cane sugar into liquid in order to refine it (remove impurities or unwanted material).

Reproduced by permission of the Library of Congress.

Childhood and youth

Henry Bessemer was born in the small town of Charlton, England, in 1813. When he was not in school, he spent time in his father's type foundry, a company that makes moveable type from metal for printing presses. Henry's father was a metallurgist (one who works with metals, refining them for various uses). He had succeeded by discovering that by adding other metals to the molten (liquefied) lead, his typefaces were harder and would not wear down as quickly after being repeatedly pressed against paper in printing presses. Even as a boy, Henry showed signs of being highly inventive. In particular, he developed a way of making three-dimensional copies in metal of artwork, such as sculptures, and everyday objects, such as flowers and leaves. When he was seventeen, Bessemer left home for London, England, where he set up his own business selling decorative metal objects.

Stamping out forgery

One of Bessemer's first inventions was praised and accepted by the British government because it solved the problem of document forgery, or illegally falsifying an official document, which was a common occurrence in England at the time. The government offices had a practice of stamping important papers, such as property deeds, to identify them as legal; unfortunately, the stamps they used were easily copied. Realizing that the government was losing significant revenue because of this problem, Bessemer invented a machine that would actually press the stamp into the paper of the document, making it more difficult to forge. An official of the Stamp Office studied Bessemer's idea for a few days and returned with a job offer: Instead of paying Bessemer for his idea, he offered him a job as superintendent of stamps.

Bessemer was thrilled. He was just twenty-one, and here was a secure government job that would give him an income sufficient to marry the girl he had been dating for two years. Excited, he took the news to his fiancée and explained his idea. She was happy at the prospect of marriage, but had a question about Bessemer's idea: Couldn't the government solve the forgery problem simply by imprinting the date on stamps?

Bessemer, somewhat embarrassed that his fiancée had so quickly come up with a simpler solution to the government's problem, felt obligated to present this new idea when he returned to the Stamp Office to start work. As it turned out, the Stamp Office liked the new idea even better; but the solution made Bessemer's services as superintendent of stamps unnecessary.

Bessemer tried for years to collect a fee from the government for the imprinting idea—after all, the government was able to collect much more revenue by preventing people from transferring old stamps—but no money was forthcoming. Bessemer had learned a basic lesson of inventors: for some people, coming up with ideas is easy, but making money from ideas is much harder.

Despite many later successes, Bessemer never got over his experience at the Stamp Office. Forty-six years later, long famous for his steelmaking process, he complained about his treatment in a letter to the *Times* of London. In response to his complaint, the government offered to make him a knight, entitled to be called *Sir* Henry Bessemer. He closely guarded his later inventions—or made sure he was protected by patents before revealing them. A patent guarantees an inventor the exclusive right to earn money from an invention, either by manufacturing an object, or using a process, or selling the rights to someone else, over a specified period of time.

Gold paint

In 1840 a printer and friend of Bessemer's, Thomas de la Rue (1793–1866; best known today for his printed playing cards), suggested that Bessemer think about a way to make gold-colored paint. It had long been the style to paint certain decorative objects, such as picture frames, so that they appeared to be made of gold. Of course, using actual gold would have been much too expensive, so the metallic effect was achieved by mixing into paint a powder made of bronze.

Bessemer discovered that the powder, which was made exclusively in Germany, was also extremely expensive. (German manufacturers had learned the technique of making the powder from those in China and Japan and had kept it secret

Welcome to Bessemer!

At least ten towns in the United States are named after Henry Bessemer, including three in Pennsylvania alone. The others are:

- Bessemer, Alabama
- Bessemer, Florida
- Bessemer, Michigan
- Bessemer, North Carolina
- Bessemer, Ohio
- Bessemer, Virginia
- Bessemer, West Virginia

to maintain their monopoly, or exclusive ownership, of the product.) Bessemer designed a machine to make the powder fairly inexpensively. Before long he was manufacturing the powder and selling it at one-eighth the price charged by the German manufacturers.

Stung by his experience at the Stamp Office, Bessemer and his family kept the gold paint process secret for thirty-five years, allowing no one to even see the machines.

Bessemer's gold paint was his first major monetary success, and his profits allowed for the establishment of his own brass foundry in London.

Artillery shells and the origin of the Bessemer process

One of Bessemer's greatest inventions was an outgrowth of the Crimean War (1853–56), in which England battled with Russia over control of the eastern Mediterranean region. Bessemer was led to develop an improved way of manufacturing steel as a result of a problem with British cannons made of cast iron. The accuracy of cannons could be improved by carving spiral-shaped grooves inside the cannon barrel, which caused the cannon balls to spin. But this process, called rifling, created another problem: in order to work, shells had to fit snugly inside the barrel, which created significant pressure against the barrel when the shells were fired. The cannon barrels were made of cast iron, which was brittle and prone to exploding, often killing the gun crew.

The solution was to use steel instead of cast iron. Both cast iron and steel are produced from iron ore, which naturally is mixed with atoms of carbon. The characteristics of the metal differ according to the percentage of carbon (it ranges from a high of around 4 percent to under 1 percent). Steel has low carbon content, and making steel requires heating a basic form of iron, called pig iron, to a high temperature so that carbon (and some other impurities, such as sulfur) mixed in

Henry Bessemer discovered that using steel in cannon barrels, instead of the traditional cast iron, greatly improved their accuracy, thus changing the face of warfare. *Reproduced by permission of Hulton/Archive.*

with the iron burns off. The result is steel, a metal that is strong, like cast iron, but not as brittle, thanks to the reduced carbon content. But as desirable as steel was for making cannon barrels, it was also very expensive to produce. Reducing the carbon content required heating a basic form of iron to an extremely high temperature, which took a significant amount of fuel (such as coal) and time. Moreover, using traditional methods, steel was produced in relatively small batches. Bessemer set about looking for ways to reduce the cost of making steel on a large scale, with the goal of substituting steel for cast iron in British cannons.

The Bessemer process

In 1856 Bessemer discovered a new process whereby steel could be made much more easily, much less expensively, and in much greater quantities. He was experimenting on a small quantity of molten (liquefied) iron when he discovered that some of it had turned into steel after oxygen was blown across the surface (done in order to raise the temperature of the molten iron). Bessemer realized that by exposing the iron to more oxygen, impurities (mostly carbon) would burn off, leaving molten steel.

The Bessemer process involved the use of a special furnace, called a Bessemer converter (depicted here), to force oxygen into liquid iron. The oxygen burned off impurities in the iron and resulted in steel. The process made steel manufacturing economical and feasible. *Reproduced by permission of the Library of Congress.*

Bessemer built on this idea by constructing a furnace with a hole through which oxygen could be forced into the molten iron. The oxygen bubbled through the furnace, burning off the impurities. It was a one-step process that could produce steel at ten times the rate of the previous process, and in much greater quantities. The special furnaces came to be called Bessemer converters. Instead of producing fifty pounds of steel at a time, Bessemer could produce sixty thousand pounds. Although others were also working on a steelmaking process, notably William Kelly (1811–1888) of the United States, Bessemer was the first to make steelmaking a profitable business.

Bessemer's invention came at the very time when the demand for a strong and durable metal, like steel, was increasing dramatically. Railroads greatly preferred steel over iron for rails, and shipbuilding and armaments were also rapidly expanding markets for steel. Within a decade, the Bessemer process accounted for all but a small fraction of the steel manufactured in England.

Bessemer and the Industrial Revolution

Bessemer had made two fortunes by the time he was fifty-three: one for gold paint and the other for steel. Along the way, he also developed new techniques for refining sugarcane and compressing powdery graphite into pencils. He also developed a telescope, a solar furnace, and equipment for polishing diamonds. However, it was his steel process that pushed the Industrial Revolution forward to make the manufacturing world what it is today. Economical steel found a wide range of uses, ranging from the girders that support skyscrapers, to many parts of automobiles and other vehicles, up to and including aircraft carriers. Steel's strength, relative light weight, and ability to be pressed into large, thin sheets made it an ideal material for a huge variety of products. It is hard to imagine the advance of the Industrial Revolution without steel.

Bessemer, widely respected and at last rewarded by the British government for his suggestion on stamps, retired a wealthy man at age fifty-six. He died in London, England, at age eighty-five on March 15, 1898.

For More Information

Books

Bessemer, Henry. *Sir Henry Bessemer, F.R.S.: An Autobiography.* London, England: Offices of Engineering, 1905; reprinted by the Institute of Metals, 1989.

Bolton, Sarah Knowles. *Lives of Poor Boys Who Became Famous.* New York: T. Y. Crowell and Co., 1885.

Burn, Duncan. *The Economic History of Steelmaking, 1867–1939.* Cambridge, England: Cambridge University Press, 1961.

Periodicals

Stone, Joseph K. "Early Advocates of the Use of Oxygen in Steelmaking." *Steel Times International,* June 2002, p. 43.

Web Sites

Hart-Davis, Adam. "Henry Bessemer, Man of Steel." *Science and Technology On-Line.* http://www2.exnet.com/1995/09/27/science/science.html (accessed on February 13, 2003).

Andrew Carnegie

Born November 25, 1835
Dunfermline, Scotland

Died August 11, 1919
Lenox, Massachusetts

Scottish-born American industrialist and philanthropist

"I would as soon leave my son a curse as the almighty dollar."

Reproduced by permission of the Library of Congress.

Andrew Carnegie's name is synonymous with the steel industry. Starting from poverty, he built an enormous fortune by utilizing a new process for making steel and creating the largest steel-manufacturing company in the United States at precisely the time the world was turning from iron to steel to build railroads, skyscrapers, machine tools, and automobiles.

Carnegie was the son of a poor Scottish weaver. After immigrating to the United States with his family, he began a swift, steady rise to overwhelming business success, living out the ultimate rags-to-riches story. Carnegie held varied and diverse jobs in his career: he was a textile factory worker, a telegraph messenger boy, a telegraph operator, a railroad supervisor and then railroad owner, and finally an owner of steel factories, with each success building upon the previous one. He brought innovation to each and every business enterprise he touched and amassed one of the largest fortunes of the late nineteenth century.

From humble origins

When Andrew Carnegie was born in 1835, his family was just a few years away from being affected by the onset of the Industrial Revolution, a period marked by the widespread replacement of manual labor by machines that began in Great Britain in the eighteenth century, although it is doubtful that they realized it at the time. His father, William, was a weaver, producing cloth on his own loom and employing three assistants in a business operated out of the family home (a so-called cottage industry). The income allowed for a decent living.

When Andrew was just eight years old, a steam-powered textile mill opened in the Carnegie's hometown of Dunfermline, Scotland, and the family's cozy existence was wiped away. The mill could produce much more cloth many times faster than a hand weaver possibly could, and the mill could sell it more cheaply. The Carnegie's income began to decline, and they grew to accept the fact that their way of life could no longer be sustained. Their solution, the same decision reached by so many others at that time, was to move to the United States.

The Carnegies settled in Pittsburgh, Pennsylvania, where they had relatives. The year was 1848, and Pittsburgh was a bustling, growing city of more than forty-thousand people, offering plenty of opportunities. Andrew's father believed that he could make a living the way he used to, and for a short while he wove tablecloths on a wooden loom and tried to sell them. When he sadly accepted that he could not support his family this way, he took a job in a textile mill, tending a power-driven loom. Andrew, who was by now thirteen years old, joined him. They both worked twelve hours per day, six days per week. Andrew was paid $1.20 a week. His father found the factory and the work to be depressing and soon quit the job, but Andrew stayed on. His wages, along with what his mother could earn sewing shoes for a nearby cobbler, kept the family alive. When Andrew had the chance to move to another factory for $2.00 per week, he gladly took it. That turned out to be the first small step in a long career of uninterrupted success.

Young Andrew Carnegie was consistently competent, cheerful, and hardworking, and people were drawn to his open, pleasant ways. At the new job, the owner took notice of him, sometimes calling Carnegie away from the factory floor to write business letters for him. Then came a piece of luck. Carnegie's uncle knew a man who was looking for a telegraph messenger boy. Carnegie was hired, at a salary of $2.50 per week. Besides delivering telegraph messages to businesses in Pittsburgh, the messenger boys were able to practice sending and receiving messages themselves if they came to the office before it officially opened for the day. Carnegie took full advantage of this opportunity to become adept at telegraphy, and soon was promoted to telegraph operator, at $25.00 per month.

For a time Carnegie was one of only a handful of operators in the country who could translate into letters the sound of a series of long and short clicks sent over telegraph wires. (American inventor **Samuel F. B. Morse** [1791–1872; see entry] had invented a code that used combinations of long and short clicks—sometimes called dots and dashes—to stand for letters of the alphabet.) The receiving instrument on early telegraphs made marks, standing for the "dots and dashes," on paper tape, which trained operators then converted back into letters. Carnegie was one of the few who could do the conversion simply by hearing the clicks, without bothering to read the marks on paper. His skill was so impressive that curious businesspeople would drop in just to see him work. Soon, business leaders were requesting that Carnegie send their important messages. One of these was Thomas A. Scott, of the Pennsylvania Railroad. In 1853 seventeen-year-old Carnegie went to work for the railroad as Scott's general assistant.

Working on the railroad

The Pennsylvania Railroad ran across the state of Pennsylvania, from Philadelphia in the east to Pittsburgh in the west. Carnegie often traveled along the line to oversee construction and maintenance projects.

On one of these trips, a stranger named Theodore Woodruff approached Carnegie about a new invention, the sleeping car. He carried a small model with him, which he showed to Carnegie. It looked like an ordinary railroad car, but the sleeping car was designed so that at night it could be converted to allow sleeping space for travelers. Carnegie realized the value of the notion and discussed it with the head of the railroad, who quickly decided to acquire the sleeping cars for the line. For his role in bringing the sleeping car to the railroad, Carnegie was allowed to buy a share in the new Woodruff Sleeping Car Company, which earned him more than $5,000 in its first year.

In 1859 Carnegie was named superintendent of the western division of the railroad. His salary was now $1,500 per year. He gained a reputation for working hard to keep the trains running on schedule. This meant pushing his work crews to keep the cast-iron rails, which were prone to breaking, in good repair. When the railroad company built its own telegraph line, Carnegie and his assistant became the first to employ women as telegraph operators, declaring that the women were more reliable than male operators.

With the outbreak of the American Civil War (1861–65), the focus of Carnegie's responsibilities changed abruptly. His knowledge of both the telegraph and railroads was highly valued. The Union Army (fighting for the Northern states) depended on good communications to move its troops and keep supplies flowing. When he wasn't out on the line, supervising track work or the rebuilding of lines, Carnegie was involved with the work of the U.S. Military Telegraph Corps. He worked himself to exhaustion; one hot day, while overseeing work on a bridge in Virginia, he suffered from sunstroke. He was so weak and tired that even he was forced to admit that he needed a vacation, so he took one—his first in almost fifteen years.

But Carnegie had not been too busy to make personal investments during the war years. He used his profits from the Woodruff Sleeping Car Company to invest in other companies, and with those profits he made more investments. When the Civil War ended, he was twenty-nine years old and owned shares in more than a dozen companies, worth a total of almost $40,000. When he was offered a promotion to general superintendent of the Pennsylvania Railroad, he turned it down in order to tend to his investments.

Determined to make a fortune

Carnegie was shrewd and forthright, a winning combination for a full-time investor. When he saw an opportunity to merge the Woodruff Sleeping Car Company with a rival, he made it happen, becoming the largest investor in the new

Pullman Palace Car Company, which promptly cornered the worldwide market for sleeping cars. Noting the delays caused by broken or burned wooden railroad bridges, he organized a company to construct cast-iron bridges.

On a trip to England, Carnegie toured a steel mill. He realized that steel, being stronger than iron, would make better, safer, longer-lasting railroad tracks. Within three years, he had built a steel mill near Pittsburgh, Pennsylvania, and was supplying steel rails to railroads. He was among the first to use an efficient, new steelmaking process developed in England by **Henry Bessemer** (1813–1898; see entry). Soon he acquired more mills, and then he bought part of a company that owned coalfields in order to guarantee that the mills would always have a steady supply of raw materials.

Carnegie was obsessed with providing his customers with the best steel at the best price. He hired scientists to study the chemistry of steelmaking, and he did not hesitate to build new plants to improve the quality of his product and the efficiency of his operations.

At the same time, he was determined to be a kind employer, dedicated to the welfare of his employees. On the other hand, Carnegie strongly resisted the efforts of steelworkers to organize into unions. This inherent conflict came to a head in 1892, when steelworkers at Carnegie's Homestead plant in Pennsylvania went on strike. While Carnegie vacationed in Scotland, he put his newly appointed chief executive, Henry Clay Frick (1849–1919), in charge. Violence broke out, and several strikers—and hired company guards—were killed.

The Homestead strike caused Carnegie great distress. The public blamed him, as the mill owner, for the tragedy, and accused him of hiding in Scotland while letting Frick do his dirty work. In truth, Carnegie was furious at the way Frick handled the crisis. Two years later, Carnegie replaced Frick with Charles Schwab (1862–1939) as chief executive; Schwab had begun his career as a common laborer.

Successful as he was, Carnegie did not stop building his company. He bought the rights to mine iron ore in the Mesabi Range of Minnesota, where ore could be scooped from just beneath the surface at a cost of merely five cents a ton, versus three dollars a ton for underground ore. In 1898

The Homestead Strike

The Homestead mill, outside of Pittsburgh, Pennsylvania, was part of the Carnegie Steel Company. In July 1892 the mill's contract with union workers was due for renewal. Carnegie was vacationing in a remote area of Scotland at the time, and Henry Clay Frick (1849–1919), the chief executive of Carnegie Steel, was in charge.

Determined to resist the workers' demands, Frick erected a high fence around the entire factory. There was barbed wire at the top and watchtowers that could hold armed men. Then he hired three hundred "guards" from the Pinkerton Detective Agency. On July 1, 1892, the Homestead workers went on strike, and the mill was shut down.

On the night of July 5, 1892, the Pinkerton guards, or "Pinks," as they were called, began arriving, riding on barges pulled by tugboats up the Monongahela River. A striker spotted the barges and raised an alarm, bringing enraged strikers rushing to the plant. Strikers ripped a hole in the fence surrounding the steel mill and streamed into the plant. With the barges docked at the company wharf, shooting broke out. Strikers even used the cannon at the town hall to fire on the barges, but the ancient weapon blew up, killing a striker.

Eventually the strikers negotiated a surrender, but union leaders could not control the enraged strikers, and three "Pinks" were killed as they retreated through the mob.

Eventually, Pennsylvania National Guard troops restored order and protected the mill. On July 23, a striker broke into Frick's office and shot him twice and stabbed him three times. Frick survived the attack, and by November 1892 the plant was operating again.

Carnegie built steamboats to carry the ore from Lake Superior to Conneaut, Ohio, on Lake Erie, and built his own railroad to haul the ore to his mills in Pittsburgh.

Even though the market for rails was diminishing in the late 1890s, new uses for steel were springing up: for steel columns in building skyscrapers and the elevators inside them, girders to build elevated tracks for city tramways, and pipes to deliver water and gas to cities.

In 1900 Carnegie Steel was the largest steel company in the world. Its production was greater than the entire production of steel in Britain. Carnegie had become the most successful man in the steel industry.

The following year, the financier **J. P. Morgan** (1837–1913; see entry) attempted to assemble a trust, a combination of corporations, in order to gain exclusive control of the steel industry. To do so, he needed Carnegie Steel. Morgan approached Schwab, the company president, and requested that he find out how much Carnegie would sell his company for. The following day, Carnegie wrote a figure on a slip of paper: $480 million. Morgan accepted the price. Shortly thereafter, Morgan organized United States Steel, with Carnegie's mills as the centerpiece. Carnegie retired from the steel business.

The philanthropist

As Carnegie entered middle age he began to pay attention to two new pursuits: his personal life and philanthropy (benefiting others through charitable gifts). He treated himself to more travel, including a nearly year-long trip around the world. He and his mother also took a triumphant and sentimental trip back to Dunfermline, Scotland, where Carnegie took one of his first steps as a philanthropist by donating a new public library to the town of his birth. In a special ceremony, Mrs. Carnegie laid the foundation stone of the new building.

It was not until the death of his mother in 1886 that Carnegie considered marriage. In 1887, at age fifty-one, he married Louise Whitfield (1857–1946), with whom he had been in love for years. It would be ten years before their only child, Margaret, was born.

At age sixty-five, with a personal fortune of roughly $360 million (worth about $8 billion in the year 2000), Carnegie set about giving it away, partly in the belief that inheriting money spoiled children. As a philanthropist, he is most remembered for the public libraries he established; the total number would eventually come to 2,811. Most of them were in the United States; every state except Rhode Island had at least one Carnegie library. It also pleased him to give organs to churches; a total of nearly five thousand of the instruments were donated in the United States, and thousands more scattered in churches throughout the world. He gave financial support to many individuals, from friends in Dunfermline to celebrities and politicians.

On a more public stage, Carnegie established pension (retirement) funds in several areas, including a fund for Carnegie Steel employees and a fund for college professors. The Hero Fund awarded prizes for acts of heroism. New York City got Carnegie Hall, which became a world-renowned concert hall. Pittsburgh was given the Carnegie Institute of Technology, and many colleges received large gifts, including the Tuskegee Institute, a school serving African Americans. Princeton University got a three-and-a-half-mile-long, man-made lake on its campus so students could participate in the sport of rowing.

Upon Andrew Carnegie's death on August 11, 1919, he was worth $23 million; he had succeeded in giving away 90 percent of his fortune.

For More Information

Books

Livesay, Harold C. *Andrew Carnegie and the Rise of Big Business.* New York: Longman, 2000.

Meltzer, Milton. *The Many Lives of Andrew Carnegie.* New York: Franklin Watts, 1997.

Wall, Joseph Frazier. *Andrew Carnegie.* Pittsburgh, PA: University of Pittsburgh Press, 1989.

Periodicals

Chernow, Ron. "Blessed Barons." *Time,* December 7, 1998, p. 74.

McCallum, John S. "Andrew Carnegie and John Pierpont Morgan: Two Businessmen to Remember." *Business Quarterly,* March 1987, p. 6.

Web Sites

Carnegie, Andrew. "The Gospel of Wealth." *American Studies at the University of Virginia.* http://xroads.virginia.edu/~DRBR/wealth.html (accessed on February 13, 2003).

Carnegie, Andrew. "The Opportunity of the United States." *Anti-Imperialism in the United States 1898–1935.* http://www.boondocksnet.com/ai/ailtexts/carn02.html (accessed on February 13, 2003).

Lorenzen, Michael. "The Sociological Reasons Behind Andrew Carnegie's Millions to Libraries." *Michigan State University.* http://www.lib.msu.edu/lorenze1/carnegie.htm (accessed on February 13, 2003).

"The Richest Man in the World: Andrew Carnegie." *PBS American Experience.* http://www.pbs.org/wgbh/amex/carnegie/ (accessed on February 13, 2003).

Henry Ford

Born July 30, 1863
Greenfield, Michigan

Died April 7, 1947
Dearborn, Michigan

American engineer, automobile manufacturer

"You can do anything if you have enthusiasm. Enthusiasm is the yeast that makes your hopes rise to the stars."

Reproduced by permission of the Library of Congress.

Henry Ford symbolized the fruits of the Industrial Revolution, a period marked by the widespread replacement of manual labor by machines, by standardizing parts and machinery and utilizing the moving assembly line to efficiently mass-produce cars. To many, he was a folk hero: from a modest beginning on a farm near Detroit, Michigan, where he attended a one-room schoolhouse, he built an enormous enterprise that was for a time the largest manufacturer of automobiles in the world. At one time, a brand-new Ford Model T cost just less than three hundred dollars, a price low enough that Ford's own workers could afford to buy one for their families. It was Henry Ford who put ordinary American workers into cars, which had previously been luxuries for the wealthy.

The moving assembly line, a highly efficient means of production in which a series of individual workers had one task to perform as each car moved down the line, came to be associated with Ford's company, and the entire process became known as the American system. It became a global model for industrialization and the economic success of the United States.

Despite his business success, Ford raised much controversy. Once praised for raising his workers' wages well above what other companies paid, he was later harshly criticized for employing company spies and armed police to prevent workers from joining the United Automobile Workers Union (UAW). He owned a newspaper that spewed religious hatred against Jews and once had words of praise for the Nazi leader Adolf Hitler (1889–1945). An avowed pacifist, someone opposed to war under any circumstances, Ford once sponsored a "peace ship" that tried to negotiate an end to World War I (1914–18); but he also employed his factories full-force to produce bombers during World War II (1939–45).

Childhood and youth

Henry Ford was born in 1863, the first of six children, on his family's farm in a settlement that is now part of Dearborn, Michigan, about nine miles from Detroit. His father, William Ford, had emigrated from Ireland in 1847, part of a massive wave of Irish immigrants following a disastrous crop failure.

Young Henry attended a one-room schoolhouse in Greenfield, Michigan. The school used books written by the American educator William McGuffey (1800–1873) to teach reading. The McGuffey *Readers* were widely used by teachers during the nineteenth century. In the process of teaching children to read, they also imparted a moral view of life and the virtues of hard work and rugged individualism. The underlying idea was that an individual could get ahead in the world by working hard. Social or economic conditions were not an excuse. It was a philosophy that Ford absorbed, coming to believe he was living proof of the lessons in the books. Later in life he acknowledged it by building a reproduction of his childhood schoolhouse, complete with McGuffey *Readers,* in his museum called Greenfield Village in Dearborn, Michigan.

Despite the virtues of hard work taught by McGuffey and experienced on the family farm, the farming life did not appeal to Ford. In his autobiography, *My Life and Work,* published in 1922, he wrote:

> There was too much hard hand labor on our own and all other farms of the time. Even when very young I suspected that

About Prices

In telling the story of Henry Ford, as well as the stories of many other people in this book, we refer to prices as they were many years ago. For example, Henry Ford sold new Model T automobiles for just less than three hundred dollars in 1927. But a dollar would buy a lot more goods in 1927 than it would in 2002, as most people realize. Just how much more?

In an effort to put prices from bygone eras into perspective, this book uses a formula provided by the U.S. Bureau of Labor Statistics to compare prices now with prices then. The formula, and the statistics used to calculate the difference, can be found on a Web site maintained by the Federal Reserve Bank of Minneapolis. The url is: http://minneapolisfed.org/research/data/us/calc/hist1800.cfm.

much might somehow be done in a better way. That is what took me into mechanics—although my mother always said that I was born a mechanic.... My father was not entirely in sympathy with my bent toward mechanics. He thought I ought to be a farmer.

Ford's mother was right: her firstborn son had a natural inclination toward machinery and engineering. As a teenager he learned to assemble watches and a working model of a self-propelled threshing machine, which is used to separate seeds or grain from the straw, he encountered when he was twelve.

At age seventeen, Ford gave up on farming and school and walked nine miles to Detroit, where he got a job at the Michigan Car Works. But after a week, he left that job for one that paid less but enabled him to work in a machine shop. He also made extra money repairing watches in the evening. An article about the recently invented internal combustion engine so excited Ford that he changed jobs again, for a chance to work at the Dry Dock Engine Company, where he worked as an apprentice, learning the basics of the trade while on the job.

For about a century, the steam engine developed by **James Watt** (1736-1819; see entry) was the chief source of energy (besides flowing water in a river or stream) for machines in factories and for mechanical transportation like railroads and steam ships. The steam engine let steam inside a cylinder in the space under a solid tubular piece of metal called the piston. As the steam expanded, it pushed the piston up in the cylinder; as soon as the source of heat was removed, steam condensed back into liquid, forming a vacuum that sucked the piston back down. A rod attached to the upper end of the piston thus moved up and down and, through a series of gears, caused wheels to turn.

The internal combustion engine worked in the same basic way, except that it substituted an explosion of burning gasoline for the expanding steam under the piston. Gasoline, a chemical derived from crude oil, was mixed with oxygen and sprayed into the cylinder, whereupon an electric spark ignited the mixture which exploded with great force, which pushed the piston up.

Internal combustion engines promised many advantages over steam engines. For one thing, they did not require a separate fire (usually burning coal) to heat water and create steam. Gasoline carried more energy per ounce (gram) than a comparable amount of coal. And there was no need for someone to tend a coal fire; the internal combustion engine worked automatically, with a part called the spark plug repeatedly igniting the gasoline. Internal combustion engines could be made in a fairly compact size and still deliver enough power to move a carriage; it seemed ideal to bring mechanical power to personal vehicles, like automobiles.

Fulfilling a dream

Ford left the Dry Dock Engine Company when his father asked him to come back home and work on the family farm. It was during this time that he began courting Clara Bryant, the daughter of a neighboring farmer. Three years later, in April 1888, he and Clara were married. She proved to be a steadfast believer in Ford's dream throughout the difficult days when he was starting his automobile business. On November 6, 1893, the Fords' only child, Edsel, was born.

Ford's father had given his son a forty-acre plot of land, where he built a home for himself and his family. Ford also built a machine shop, and he spent his spare time drawing plans to build a gasoline-powered internal combustion engine. Karl Benz (1844–1929) of Germany had already demonstrated a car propelled by an internal combustion engine in 1885, and by the time Ford entered the business, many other auto pioneers were already turning out models of their own. Ford's main idea was to make a car so inexpensive that ordinary people could afford to buy one; whereas his early competitors viewed cars as luxury items for the wealthy.

In 1891 Ford again moved from the farm to Detroit—for good, this time—to pursue his dream of building a car with his engine design. It was a time when most people got around town by walking, riding horses, or traveling in buggies pulled by horses.

In the city, Ford got a job as a machinist, and equipped his own small machine shop in a shed behind the house in which he and his family lived on Bagley Avenue. He tested his first engine in 1893. It was a somewhat crude experiment: the spark plug, which is the part of an engine that creates a spark that causes a mixture of gasoline and oxygen to ignite, was powered by a cord connected to a socket in the house. (Later, a battery was used for this purpose.) But it worked. Ford now turned to the task that would make him famous: using the engine to propel a vehicle.

Ford's first working model

In 1896 Ford cut a hole in the wall of his shed and drove his first "car" onto the street. He called it the *Quadricycle,* because it had four wheels instead of two, like a bicycle. It consisted of a fuel tank with a seat bolted on top, an internal combustion engine that Ford had built, and four bicycle wheels. The Quadricycle was noisy—horses were startled by it—and uncomfortable, but it ran successfully. Ford sold the Quadricycle and used the money to develop a new and better model.

To earn a living at the time, Ford worked for the Detroit Edison Illuminating Company. There he met the famous inventor Thomas Edison (1847–1931), who admired Ford's work. Edison is said to have told Ford: "Young man, you have it, a self-contained unit carrying its own fuel. Keep at it!" Whether literally true or not, Ford became a close friend of Edison's.

Ford's bosses at Detroit Edison admired his work on cars but felt that he was spending too much time on his hobby at the expense of his job. They asked him to make a choice: a secure career as general superintendent at Detroit Edison, or making cars. For Ford, the choice was inevitable: he chose cars.

Henry Ford demonstrates his first car, the Quadricycle, in 1896. *Reproduced by permission of the American Automobile Manufacturers Association.*

Henry Ford, car manufacturer

Ford did not invent the automobile or the internal combustion engine. He did, however, design a working self-propelled machine that used a gasoline engine. He also founded the company that still bears his name and developed new methods of manufacturing that drove down the cost of his cars so that ordinary working people could afford to own one.

His success in business did not come instantly, however. With the backing of several investors, he formed the Detroit Automobile Company in 1899; it was later renamed the Henry Ford Company. But his backers grew impatient with Ford, who insisted on constantly improving his car without manufacturing any to sell. They eventually abandoned him, and he himself left the Henry Ford Company in 1902; it later was reorganized and renamed the Cadillac Motor Car Company.

Finally, in 1903, Ford formed the Ford Motor Company. To do so, he raised $28,000 in cash from ordinary citizens,

The Model T changed the face of the automobile industry by making a car available to the mass population at an affordable price. *Reproduced by permission of AP/Wide World Photos.*

having previously annoyed most of the wealthy individuals of Detroit who had invested in his earlier enterprises. It was during this year that Ford introduced his first model: the Model A. From a factory on Mack Avenue in Detroit, Ford produced a small volume of cars. Two or three workers produced each car from parts ordered from other firms as Ford continued to introduce new models. By 1908 the factory was turning out about one hundred cars per day, and the company investors were thrilled.

But Ford had a much larger dream: he wanted to reach a productivity level of one thousand cars per day. The big break came in 1908 with his ninth model: the Model T.

When he unveiled the Model T in October 1908, Ford declared: "I will build a motor car for the great multitude"; and so he did. Over the next nineteen years, the Ford Motor Company sold more than fifteen million cars in the United States, almost a million more in Canada, and a quarter of a million in

Britain. The total production of Ford cars amounted to about half the world's cars during that period.

Ford's achievement was not just selling a lot of cars. Through constant innovation in the manufacturing process, he drove down the price of the Model T from $950 in 1908 to $280 in 1927. (In today's dollars, the price went from about $19,000 to about $3,000.) The low prices for the Model T made it possible for ordinary workers to buy one, which resulted in not only a high sales volume for the Ford Motor Company but also a profound change in the car industry. Because of Henry Ford, cars became practical for everyone, instead of a luxury reserved for the wealthy.

The Model T

Henry Ford's Model T was the first car produced for a mass market, and it was one of the most successful cars ever manufactured. Between 1909 and 1927, Ford produced fifteen million Model Ts; in 1914 alone, Ford produced 308,162, more than the total of all of the other 299 U.S. car manufacturers combined.

Production of the Model T symbolized advances in industrial production pioneered by Henry Ford. In 1913, after five years of producing the car, the time required to assemble a Model T had dropped from twelve hours and eight minutes to one hour and thirty-three minutes. To achieve this, Ford hired supervisors to constantly monitor every step in the process in order to increase worker productivity and drive down the production costs.

Although Henry Ford famously said that customers could buy a Model T in any color so long as it was black, in fact black was not even offered before 1913. The first Model Ts came in green, red, blue, and gray.

Henry Ford, social innovator

Six years after introducing the Model T, Ford introduced another innovation that was perhaps even more startling. In 1914 he offered to pay his workers five dollars per day—more than twice the average daily salary paid by other companies. Moreover, he reduced the working day from nine hours to eight hours, which allowed the company to run three shifts to keep up with demand for the Model T. (Adjusted for inflation, Ford's $5.00-a-day salary in 1914 was worth about $89.50 in 2002 for eight hours of work, or $11.18 an hour, still about twice the minimum wage.)

This action made Ford a hero to workers. Some people praised him as a great humanitarian. Others concluded that he was a madman, or worse, a socialist (one who believes in a political system where workers control businesses and the government).

Behind this action lay a character trait that helped build his company in the early years, but later radically changed the world's opinion. Ford was a stubborn man who insisted on doing things his way. His financial backers had learned that, and he continued to exercise his strong opinions on what was best, both for the Ford Motor Company and for his employees, even for the United States as a nation.

In 1918 Ford ran for the U.S. Senate at the request of President Woodrow Wilson (1856–1924), but he lost in a close election. The next year Ford lost a lawsuit in which stockholders had complained that he did not distribute enough of the company's profits in the form of dividends (stockholder's share of profits). The Supreme Court of Michigan ordered the company to pay shareholders $19 million in dividends. Furious, Ford threatened to quit the company and start another one. The price of shares in his company began falling, and Ford arranged for shares to be bought at greatly reduced prices. This allowed him to gain complete control of his company, and Ford was said to have danced a jig when the last stock transfer agreement was signed on July 11, 1919.

In the mid-1920s Ford's golden touch in the automobile business lost some of its power. Sales of the Model T began to fall, despite constantly declining prices. Whereas Ford had once boasted that for the Model T, "Any customer can have a car painted any color that he wants, so long as it is black," in the 1920s, Ford started offering the famous Tin Lizzie (nicknamed so because it used lightweight sheet metal for the body) in green, brown, or blue, as well as black. Finally, in 1928, Ford introduced a new model, dubbed the Model A, like his company's very first offering. But the Model A never rivaled the Model T; four years after its introduction, it lost out to the new and more powerful eight-cylinder engine offered by Ford's main competitors, General Motors and Chrysler. The days when Ford dominated the automobile industry were essentially over, even though his company remained—and continues to remain in the twenty-first century—a vital competitor.

A reputation tarnished

Henry Ford became wealthy as a car maker, and he sometimes dabbled in other areas, where his reputation was severely tarnished.

In 1919, he sued the *Chicago Tribune* for libel (publishing false information that harmed his reputation). The paper had printed an article accusing Ford of sympathizing with Germany during World War I, even as the United States was at war with Germany. During the trial, a lawyer for the newspaper subjected Ford to a cross-examination (questions) that showed Ford had a minimal education and knew little about subjects unrelated to making cars. He won the suit, though, and was rewarded six cents.

A few years later, in 1926, he established a newspaper of his own, the *Dearborn Independent* in Michigan, which started printing anti-Semitic (anti-Jewish) articles so extreme that some libraries and newsstands refused to carry the paper. A Jewish lawyer from Chicago and prominent organizer of farmers, Aaron Sapiro, sued Ford for libel, claiming the newspaper hurt his reputation among farmers. Ford's defense was that he had not written articles signed by him; indeed, he said he did not even read the newspaper. Ford reached a secret settlement with Sapiro, publicly apologized for any harm he might have caused, and stopped publishing the paper.

Nevertheless, the charge of anti-Semitism stuck to Ford for many years afterward, and it was renewed in 1938 when, on his seventy-fifth birthday, Ford accepted the Grand Cross of the German Eagle, the highest medal that Nazi Germany could bestow on a foreigner, from the government of Adolf Hitler. It was one of many awards from other countries that Ford accepted, but when Hitler's genocidal campaign (attempt to annihilate a race of people) against Jews in the 1930s and 1940s, known as the Holocaust, became known, the old articles in Ford's newspaper again became controversial, and his association with Hitler and the Nazi regime was widely condemned.

Labor trouble

Whereas Ford was hailed as a hero in 1914 when he voluntarily raised the pay of his workers to $5.00 a day, it was a different story in 1932. With the country in economic depression, Ford decided to cut wages from $7.00 a day to $4.00, which was actually less than what other car makers were paying. Workers also complained that the company secretly investigated the private lives of its employees and fired

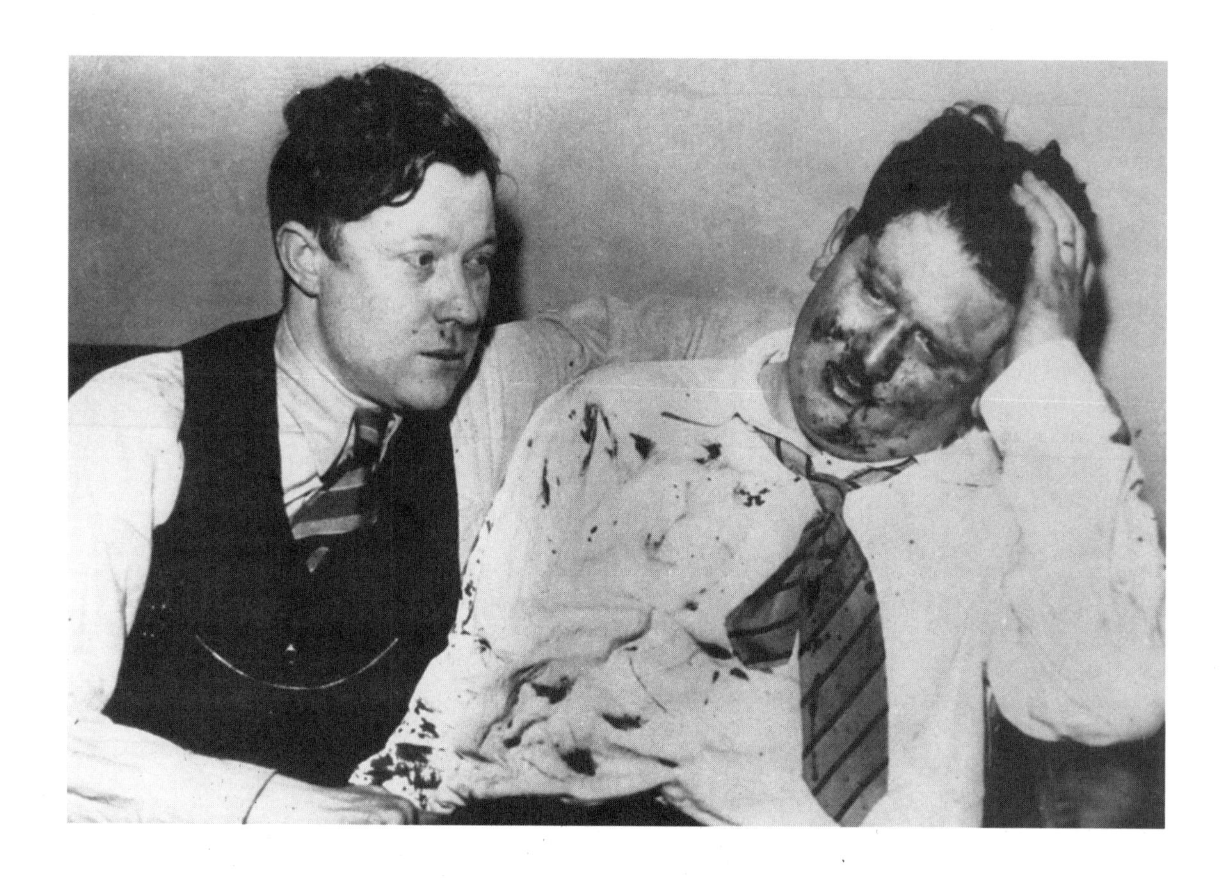

Labor leaders Richard T. Frankenstein (left) and Walter Reuther in the aftermath of a physical confrontation with security forces of the Ford Motor Company in 1937. Henry Ford fiercely resisted efforts by his workers to form unions, and Ford was the last of the large American automakers to recognize union contracts. *Reproduced by permission of the Corbis Corporation.*

workers who were found to engage in activities that were unacceptable to Ford, such as smoking, drinking, and being politically active.

Ford workers tried to join the United Automobile Workers Union (UAW), but Henry Ford employed labor spies and company police in a long effort to weed out union organizers and discourage his employees from joining a union. Like many business owners, Ford did not want his hands tied on issues of how much to pay workers, or how long they should work. Long after his major competitors, General Motors and Chrysler, had signed contracts with the union, Ford resisted. It was not until 1941 that the UAW finally signed a labor contract with the Ford Motor Company. Unions, in his mind, went against his philosophy of rugged individualism, relying on the collective instead. The union's victory came only after the National Labor Relations Board ordered the company to hold an election, in which 70 percent of Ford workers voted in favor of being represented by a union.

In his later years, Ford expressed contempt for unions. "There is nothing that a union membership could do for our people," he said. But his employees, who once hailed Ford as a hero, now complained that they had to work too fast and under great tension. "We make no attempt to coddle the people who work with us. It is absolutely a give-and-take relationship," Ford declared.

Henry Ford and the Industrial Revolution

In his life, Henry Ford came to symbolize the best and worst of the Industrial Revolution, a period of fast-paced economic change that began in Great Britain in the middle of the eighteenth century. Putting his mechanical genius to work on the issue of efficient production, Ford utilized the moving assembly line, which made possible enormous savings in the cost of making a car.

On the other hand, he himself ascribed the success of his process to "the reduction of the necessity for thought on the part of the worker, and the reduction of the movement to a minimum. He [the worker on an assembly line] does as nearly as possible only one thing with only one movement.... He must have every second necessary but not a single unnecessary second." It was the very definition of drudgery, and it laid the basis for speeding up work to the limit of human endurance, a complaint often voiced by Ford's workers. But by offering his workers an unheard-of $5.00 per day in 1914, he showed the way to sharing some of the wealth generated by industrial enterprises, made his own automobiles affordable to his workers, and profoundly influenced the course of life for the working class in the United States for the rest of the twentieth century. As social commentator Will Rogers (1879–1935) said, "It will take a hundred years to tell whether he helped us or hurt us, but he certainly didn't leave us where he found us."

In 1943 Ford's son, Edsel, the president of Ford Motor Company at the time, died suddenly of pancreatic cancer. Henry Ford, at the age of eighty, immediately stepped in and resumed active leadership of the company. But by that time, the elderly Ford had already suffered two strokes; after two years he appointed his grandson, Henry Ford II, president of the company. Two years after that, on April 7, 1947, Henry Ford died at his home in Dearborn.

For More Information

Books

Aird, Hazel B. *Henry Ford: Young Man with Ideas.* New York: Simon & Schuster, 1986.

Alvarado, Rudolph, and Sonya Alvarado. *Drawing Conclusions on Henry Ford.* Ann Arbor, MI: University of Michigan Press, 2001.

Batchelor, Ray. *Henry Ford, Mass Production, Modernism, and Design.* Manchester, U.K., and New York: Manchester University Press, 1994.

Ford, Henry. *My Life and Work.* North Stratford, NH: Ayer Co., 1999, 1922.

Gelderman, Carol. *Henry Ford: The Wayward Capitalist.* New York: Dial Press, 1981.

Gourley, Catherine. *Wheels of Time: A Biography of Henry Ford.* Brookfield, CT: Millbrook Press, 1997.

Middleton, Haydn. *Henry Ford: The People's Carmaker (What's Their Story).* New York: Oxford University Press Children's Books, 1998.

Periodicals

Halberstam, David. "Citizen Ford." *American Heritage,* October-November, 1986, p. 49.

Wamsley, James S. "Henry Ford's Amazing Time Machine." *American History Illustrated,* April 1985, p. 28.

Web Sites

"The Ford Model T: A Short History of Ford's Innovation." *United Auto Workers Local 387.* http://www.local387.org/ford_model_t.htm (accessed on February 13, 2003).

Gross, Daniel. *Forbes Greatest Business Stories of All Time.* New York: J. Wiley and Sons, 1996. Excerpts found at http://www.wiley.com/legacy/products/subject/business/forbes/ford.html (accessed on February 13, 2003).

"A Science Odyssey: People and Discoveries—Henry Ford." *Public Broadcasting Service.* http://www.pbs.org/wgbh/aso/databank/entries/btford.html (accessed on February 13, 2003).

Robert Fulton

Born November 14, 1765
Little Britain, Pennsylvania

Died February 24, 1815
New York, New York

American engineer, inventor

Robert Fulton was an American engineer and inventor who developed the first commercially successful steamboat, or a boat powered by steam, thereby transforming the transportation and travel industries and speeding up the Industrial Revolution, a period of fast-paced economic change that began in Great Britain in the middle of the eighteenth century.

As a child, Fulton enjoyed building mechanical devices, taking on such projects as rockets and a hand-propelled paddle wheel boat. His interest turned to art as he matured, and at the age of twenty-one, Fulton left the United States to study painting in England. Although he managed some success, the general response his work received was disappointing and convinced him to concentrate on his engineering skills. He spent a number of years designing a canal system in Europe and later worked on a concept for a submarine. But his fame was guaranteed by the *Clermont,* the first practical steamship, which he designed and built in 1807 to navigate the Hudson River.

By succeeding at building his steamships in the early years of the United States, Fulton made a dramatic contribu-

"What, sir? You would make a ship sail against the wind and currents by lighting a bonfire under her decks? I pray you excuse me. I have no time to listen to such nonsense.

—Napoléon Bonaparte, emperor of France, reacting to Fulton's proposal for a steamboat.

Reproduced by permission of the Library of Congress.

tion to the advancement of the Industrial Revolution. Steam-powered ships changed the nature of global commerce by making travel by sea much faster and more reliable. This made it possible for factories in Europe (especially in England) to ship goods to North America and expand their markets, just as American farms and factories could ship goods to Europe.

Childhood and youth

Robert Fulton was born in 1765. His father, also named Robert, had immigrated to the English colony of Pennsylvania from Northern Ireland. In 1759 Robert Fulton Sr. married Mary Smith of Oxford, Pennsylvania, and they raised three daughters and a son, Robert, on a 364-acre farm on Conowingo Creek, in the town of Little Britain, Pennsylvania, west of Philadelphia. When Robert was just three years old his father died, leaving the Fulton children living in relative poverty.

Young Robert was taught at home until he was eight years old, after which he attended a school run by Caleb Johnson, a strict and conservative Quaker (also known as the Society of Friends, an English religious movement) and Tory. (In Fulton's time, a Tory was someone conservative in politics who opposed the growing move for American independence from Britain.) Although Fulton would prove to be brilliant later in life, his talents were not obvious in his early schooling. He was more interested in painting and in what mechanics were doing in their nearby shops than in what Caleb Johnson was trying to teach him.

When he was seventeen years old, Fulton left home and went to Philadelphia, Pennsylvania, which was a sophisticated center of learning and the arts. It was an exciting environment for a curious and intelligent young man, and Fulton thrived. He pursued his childhood interest of painting and earned a living by creating miniature portraits, which were in some ways the equivalent of photographs in an era before photography was invented.

One person whose portrait Fulton painted was Benjamin Franklin (1706–1790), perhaps Philadelphia's best-known citizen and a leader of the American independence movement. Franklin encouraged Fulton to go to England to perfect his trade as a painter, as Franklin had done as a young man to perfect his trade as a printer. Before leaving for England, Fulton bought an 840-acre farm in the town of Hopewell, Pennsylvania, for his widowed mother. She lived there until her death in 1799, as did Fulton's sister Elizabeth, also a widow, and Elizabeth's daughter.

Off to England

In 1786, at the age of twenty-one, Fulton moved to London, England, with the intention of pursuing a career as an artist. He had little money, but he did have a letter of introduction from Benjamin Franklin to a successful American painter working in London, Benjamin West (1738–1820), who also happened to be from Pennsylvania.

Fulton worked as a painter for five years. In 1791 his work was exhibited in the Royal Gallery. Thanks, perhaps, to introductions by West, Fulton obtained several commissions to paint portraits of English aristocrats. Despite his relative success as a painter, the general response his work received was disappointing and convinced him to concentrate on his engineering skills.

A new career

Fulton began working at designing canals, artificial waterways that were often dug to connect two rivers, at a time when canal building was expanding rapidly in England. After several years of work, Fulton devised a system to help boats move from one level of a canal to a higher (or lower) level, such as when a canal was moving over a hill, for which he was granted a British patent in 1794. He also developed a series of inventions using mechanical power to dig canals, as well as a plan to use cast iron in building aqueducts, or channels of water. In 1796, he published a summary of his ideas on improving canal navigation in his *Treatise on the Improvement of Canal Navigation*.

Moving to France

Having made little progress in building canals in England, Fulton decided to try his luck in France in 1797. He began working on other projects as well, including one for fireproofing houses and another for exploding gunpowder underwater. He also developed a plan for an experimental submarine that could plant underwater mines without being detected. The submarine, or "plunging boat," as it was called, caught the eye of Robert Livingston (1746–1813), then a wealthy American ambassador to France and the owner of a twenty-year monopoly on steam navigation in New York State. Fulton shared some of his own ideas about steam power with Livingston, and Livingston agreed to provide the financing for Fulton to develop a working steamboat. If Fulton succeeded, the two would become business partners. Fulton, always in search of financing for his schemes, agreed and got to work.

Steamboat success

A practical steam engine, a machine that converts the heat energy of steam into mechanical energy by means of a piston moving in a cylinder, was developed by Scottish engineer **James Watt** (1736–1819; see entry) in 1769. By the turn of the nineteenth century, steam engines had rapidly come into use. Steam engines were so bulky and heavy, however, that they were used only as stationary power sources until John Fitch (1743–1798) made the first successful trial of a forty-five-foot steam-powered boat in 1787.

In Paris, Fulton spent two and a half years working on his own design for a steamboat. One of his test models sank when a storm caused it to toss violently, and the steam engine plunged through the boat to the bottom of the River Seine. But in August 1803, Fulton succeeded in demonstrating a new model. According to H.W. Dickinson's 1913 work *Robert Fulton: Engineer and Artist*, a French newspaper at the time described it as follows:

> During the past two or three months there has been seen at the end of the quay Chaillot a boat of curious appearance, equipped with two large wheels mounted on an axle like a cart, while behind these wheels was a kind of large stove with a pipe, as if there was some kind of a small fire engine [steam engine] intended to operate the wheels of the boat.... At six o'clock in the evening, assisted by three persons only, [the builder] put his boat in motion with two other boats in tow behind it, and for an hour and a half he afforded the curious spectacle of a boat

Robert Fulton's steamship *Clermont* was the first commercially successful steamboat. *Reproduced by permission of the Corbis Corporation.*

> moved by wheels like a cart, these wheels being provided with paddles or flat plates and being moved by a fire engine.
>
> In following it along the quay the speed against the current of the Seine appeared to us about that of a rapid pedestrian, that is about 2400 *toises* [a French measurement equivalent to about 2.2 miles] per hour; while in going down stream it was more rapid.

Flush with success, Fulton set about making a larger boat that would be commercially feasible. He was now forty-one years old, and although he had met many influential people, he had not earned a fortune. He was, however, beginning to make a name for himself. He received an offer from the administration of President Thomas Jefferson (1743–1826) to develop canals in the region acquired from France in 1803 through the Louisiana Purchase (an area extending roughly from the Mississippi River to the Rocky Mountains). But Fulton was entirely focused on the steamboat, as he explained in a letter to the secretary of war in turning down the canal project in 1811:

> I now have Ship Builders, Blacksmiths, and Carpenters occupied at New York in building and executing the machinery of my Steam Boat, and I must return to that City in ten days to direct the work till finished.... The enterprise is of much importance to me individually and I hope will be of great use in facilitating the navigation of some of our long rivers. Like every enthusiast, I have no doubt of success. I therefore work with ardor, and when adjusting the parts of the machine I cannot leave the men for a day.

Upon completion of the project, Fulton named his steamship the *Clermont,* after Robert Livingston's estate in New York. The ship was actually built by an established shipbuilder in New York, and it used a steam engine purchased from James Watt's company in England. On August 17, 1807, the *Clermont* was launched, four and a half years after Fulton entered into his agreement with Livingston in Paris. The next month, the first commercial trip was launched, at a cost of $7.00 one way. The service ran for two months until ice in the river became a problem in mid-November of that year.

Fulton obtained a patent (guaranteeing an inventor the exclusive right to earn money from an invention) for his ship in 1809, as well as an exclusive license from the state of New York to operate steamboat transportation on the Hudson River. Neither his patent nor his license deterred competitors from building similar ships and launching service up the Hudson. Fulton eventually won legal battles over his patent, but in 1825, a U.S. court ruled that he could not have the business all to himself.

Fulton's success led him to build other successively larger boats and to experiment with new designs. Competitors rushed in with their own designs, and soon steamboats were used as river ferries and to carry passengers and freight along the shores of Long Island Sound from New York to New Haven, Connecticut.

The impact of Robert Fulton

As with most inventions, that of the steamboat was not the work of any one man or of any one nation. While Fulton's name will always be associated with its evolution, he was only the last in a series of individuals inspired to apply steam power to transportation. Fulton, more than any other individual, succeeded in bringing mechanical power to ships, just as others had brought steam power to manufacturing fabric, pumping water from mines, and farming. Steam applied to transportation opened up new economic opportunities and freed people from total dependence upon the wind and weather, which had restricted water transportation since the days of the first sailing vessel.

Within a decade, in 1819, the American ship *Savannah* claimed to be the first steamship to cross the Atlantic Ocean, even though the vessel had sails and relied on wind power for a good deal of the journey. Fulton's invention, and later improvements, made crossing the Atlantic faster and less dangerous than voyages in sailing ships. By so doing, steamships facilitated the shipment of manufactured goods and raw materials between Europe and North America, and eventually around the world.

Fulton died in New York on February 24, 1815, of complications from a chest cold he had caught during a journey to New Jersey. Businesses in New York closed for a day in his honor.

For More Information

Books

Morgan, John Smith. *Robert Fulton.* New York: Mason/Charter, 1977.

Philip, Cynthia Owen. *Robert Fulton, A Biography.* New York: F. Watts, 1985.

Sale, Kirkpatrick. *The Fire of His Genius: Robert Fulton and the American Dream.* New York: Free Press, 2001.

Periodicals

Philip, Cynthia Owen. "Adventurer Armed with Fortitude." *American History Illustrated,* December 1986, p. 8.

"Robert Fulton." *American Heritage,* May–June, 1991, p. 74.

Web Sites

Dickinson, H. W. "Robert Fulton: Engineer and Artist." *Steam Engine Library, University of Rochester.* http://www.history.rochester.edu/steam/dickinson (accessed on February 13, 2003).

Fulton, Robert. "A Treatise on the Improvement of Canal Navigation." *University of Rochester.* http://www.history.rochester.edu/canal/bib/fulton/1796/ (accessed on March 3, 2003).

"Fulton, Robert." *Yahooligans Directory.* http://www.yahooligans.com/science_and_nature/machines/inventions/inventors/Fulton__Robert/ (accessed on February 13, 2003).

"Robert Fulton." *Virtuology.com.* http://www.robertfulton.org/ (accessed on February 13, 2003).

Sutcliffe, Alice Crary. *Robert Fulton and the Clermont.* New York: Century Company, 1999. http://www.ulster.net/hrmm/diglit/sutcliffe/chapter 4-5.html (accessed on January 9, 2003).

Thurston, Robert H. "Robert Fulton: His Life and Its Results." *Steam Engine Library, University of Rochester.* http://www.history.rochester.edu/steam/thurston/fulton/ (accessed on February 13, 2003).

Samuel Gompers

Born January 27, 1850
London, England

Died December 13, 1924
San Antonio, Texas

English-born American labor leader

Samuel Gompers, longtime leader of the American Federation of Labor, an organization of trade unions, had an enormous influence on the direction of the organized labor movement in the United States. As much as any single individual, he steered organized labor away from European-style socialism (the philosophy that government should own, or at least control, business activities) to focus instead on unionism (forming associations of workers who negotiate with business owners for higher wages and improved working conditions) "pure and simple," with a concentration on issues like shorter hours and higher pay. At the same time, he was largely responsible for the alignment of organized labor with the U.S. Democratic Party for most of the twentieth century.

Samuel Gompers is the name most closely associated with the rise of organized labor in the United States, but during his career as a union organizer, he was only one of many people actively working on behalf of the welfare of people employed in the rapidly growing industrial sector of the American economy. His influence was major, not just on the lives of workers but on the way that organized labor has in-

"Conscious that we are right in our movement to secure better conditions for the workers; conscious that we are entitled to it, to a continual larger share of the ever-increasing production and the productivity of the laborer, we shall continue the struggle for better homes and better surroundings."

Reproduced by permission of the Library of Congress.

fluenced business and government policy since the end of the nineteenth century.

Childhood and youth

Samuel Gompers was born in London, England, the son of Sarah Rood and cigar maker Solomon Gompers. Both Sarah and Solomon had come to England from Holland. Samuel was sent to a Jewish school until he was about ten, but the family was too poor to keep Samuel in school. At first he became an assistant to a bootmaker, in order to learn the trade, and later to a cigar maker, following his father's footsteps.

In 1863 Solomon and Sarah decided that their family's future would be brighter in the United States. The family left England and landed in New York, where Solomon and Samuel resumed their careers making cigars. They lived on Manhattan's Lower East Side, which was then a bustling community of European immigrants attracted to the rapidly expanding industrial economy of post–Civil War (1861–65) New York.

After helping his father for a few months in New York, Samuel, who was just thirteen at the time, got a job as a cigar maker and in 1864 joined the Cigarmakers' Union. It did not seem like a momentous step at the time. "All my life, I had been accustomed to the labor movement and accepted as a matter of course that every wage-earner should belong to the union of his trade," he wrote in his memoirs, *Seventy Years of Life and Labor,* many years later. Unions are associations of workers who joined together to negotiate with business owners for higher pay and better working conditions. Individual workers had little chance of influencing a company, but if all a company's workers came together to present the same demands, employers were more likely to listen and agree.

For young Samuel, in addition to being a career, making cigars was also an education: the custom among cigar makers was to assign one individual the job of reading books and magazines to others in the room. Some of the rolled cigars would be set aside to compensate the reader for the time he spent reading (cigar makers were paid by the cigar rather than by the hour). Though not in a traditional classroom, it was as a reader that Gompers rounded out his education.

Gompers was a good reader and was often chosen by his colleagues for that task. In turn, he shared his own evolving thoughts about economic organization and ways to improve the living conditions of working people. In addition to reading newspapers and magazines to his colleagues, Gompers (and other readers) also acquired and read the writing of political philosophers such as **Karl Marx** (1818–1883; see entry) and other European socialists, those who advocated that working people take control of the government and pass laws to protect workers (or, in some cases, to seize ownership of factories and run them for the benefit of everyone, not just the owners).

Getting involved with unions

The last quarter of the nineteenth century was a time of social change in the United States, as well as in Europe. On the one hand, the Industrial Revolution, a period marked by the widespread replacement of manual labor by machines that began in Great Britain in the middle of eighteenth century, was gaining momentum with the rapid expansion of the U.S. population. The major business figures of the U.S. Industrial Revolution, such as **John D. Rockefeller** (1839–1937), **J. P. Morgan** (1837–1913), **Andrew Carnegie** (1835–1919), and **Jay Gould** (1836–1892; see entries), among many others, were organizing and building giant industrial enterprises to drill and refine oil, manufacture steel, and build transcontinental railroads. Large numbers of Europeans were migrating to the United States, taking low-paying jobs in the new factories and enterprises. Tensions developed between business owners and the new immigrants as a result of this rapid economic expansion. The workers wanted to be paid more for their effort; the business owners wanted to pay as little as possible.

In the 1880s and even into the 1890s, Gompers followed the ideas of socialists, particularly Karl Marx, closely. At the time Marx was the leading theorist of European socialism; he advocated the violent overthrow of governments and a takeover by workers of private property, a system he called communism. Marx also believed that property owners and workers were natural enemies, a phenomenon he called class warfare.

But while Gompers may have supported the theories of class warfare, which implies that one class would eventually triumph over the other, he always maintained a practical focus and worked to obtain concrete improvements in the lives of members of the Cigarmakers' Union. Among his fellow cigar makers were socialists who had emigrated from Europe to the United States, notably a man from Sweden, Ferdinand Laurrell, whom Gompers met and later considered a teacher.

Starting in 1875, Laurrell joined Gompers and union leader Adolph Strasser to rebuild the union, which had lost strength. According to Gompers, it was Laurrell who stressed building the strength of the union to represent cigar makers in negotiations with employers, rather than focusing on changing government policy towards business in general, as socialists advocated. Trade unions, Gompers came to believe, should focus on specific benefits for workers—higher pay and shorter hours were the two most important—whereas socialism was more all-encompassing and tended to focus on how the working class could gain control of the government. Laurrell urged Gompers to take lessons from the socialists, but to resist joining them. Gompers took the advice.

The rise of trade unionism

Gompers's role was as president of the local chapter of the Cigarmakers' Union, while Strasser became the union's international president, a title that more expressed wishful thinking than reality since the union had no members outside of the United States. Together, they achieved four goals. First, they insisted that leaders of local chapters should take orders from the international officers of the union. Second, they greatly increased union dues in order to provide the union with the ability to finance its activities, including strikes. Third, they put national officers in charge of the union's funds. And fourth, they designed a variety of benefits for union members, such as replacing lost wages if a worker became ill, had an accident, or lost a job.

In their vision, the union became a central institution in the lives of its members. The union, not the government (as the socialists advocated), would take care of its members during hard times, even providing workers with financial assistance when necessary. The union also was responsible for representing workers in talks with employers about financing benefits and negotiating for a higher pay.

Under the leadership of Gompers and Strasser, the Cigarmakers' Union became the model for other unions in the United States. By the 1890s, when the U.S. economy experienced a severe downturn, the Cigarmakers' Union had built up enough economic strength by collecting and managing members' dues to help protect its members from the worst effects of a slow economy.

Gompers's contribution went well beyond his work with the Cigarmakers' Union. In 1881 he helped establish the Federation of Organized Trades and Labor Unions of the United States and Canada, a group of unions representing skilled workers. (Skilled workers usually underwent several years of training to do their jobs; examples included cigarmakers, carpenters or brick layers.) Five years later, this organization was succeeded by the American Federation of Labor (AFL), which still exists as part of the AFL-CIO (a combination of the original AFL and the Congress of Industrial Organizations, founded in 1935), the largest affiliation of labor unions in the United States in 2002. In 1886 Gompers became president of the newly formed AFL, an office he held for the rest of his life, except for one year when a rival was elected president.

Gompers did not start out with a vision of trade unionism and then stick with it for the rest of his life. Over time, his views changed as circumstances changed. For example, when he started working, cigar making was a highly skilled craft, learned over years of practice as an apprentice (assistant). With time, manufacturers introduced the mold, which reduced the need for workers skilled in rolling tobacco leaves into cigars, and other aspects of automation. At first, Gompers resisted the introduction of machines as a threat to the livelihood of his union members; later, he came to accept the inevitability of some automation and fought to obtain a share of its benefits for his members as well as for employers.

In the beginning, Gompers was an advocate of equal rights for all workers, notably including African Americans. Later, Gompers assumed more conservative positions and was less adamant about racial equality. Gompers had started as a

A cigar maker is rendered homeless after suddenly losing his job. Samuel Gompers sought to protect the rights of workers by strengthening the role of trade unions. *Reproduced by permission of the Library of Congress.*

skilled craftsman, most of whom were whites at the time, and his union activities continued to reflect the interests of skilled workers, as opposed to unskilled workers who were paid an hourly wage for tending to a machine. For many decades, there was a distinction between the two sets of workers—reflected today in the name AFL-CIO: the AFL is an alliance of unions representing skilled workers, whereas the CIO is an alliance of unions representing employees in specific industries (United Steelworkers, for example) regardless of individual skills.

The central idea for Gompers was that the trade union, not the government or any other organization, should play the main role in representing the rights and economic demands of its members. He insisted that trade unions become central to workers' lives, and he believed that there could be only one national union (having several local chapters) for each craft. Gompers also insisted that the national union have the last word in negotiating contracts for workers and in other important issues.

Moreover, Gompers felt strongly that economic issues were the only issues that unions should deal with. He recognized that working people came from all races, all nationalities, and all religions, but pointed out that what all union members had in common was their concern for economic prosperity: how much money they earned an hour, how many hours they were required to work, their rights as workers.

Gompers resisted other aspects of union organization, such as setting up buying cooperatives, or organizations of people who negotiate better prices by purchasing for the group rather than individually, or commonly owned businesses. Union members were workers and should focus on what they knew how to do well, rather than stray into areas of business where they lacked expertise, he insisted.

There were two sides to this aspect of Gompers's philosophy. On the one hand, he insisted on limiting union involvement to economic issues that directly affected union members. On the other hand, he was willing to concede to business management its role in running a business. Thus, he moved away from the idea of class warfare, which implies that one class would eventually triumph over the other, and instead turned trade unionism into a kind of exchange of equals. Working people would negotiate for the biggest share of the economic pie they could achieve and leave running the business to professional management.

Gompers, unions, and politics

In the early years of the 1900s, both Democrats and Republicans vied for the votes of workers. The Democratic Party continued to be associated with the more conservative states of the American South and the defeated Confederacy of the U.S. Civil War (1861–65). The Republicans were more closely aligned with the industrial interests of the North. Both parties competed for the votes of the working people (as distinct from the landowning class or business owners) in the growing industrial economy.

The labor movement initially resisted affiliation with political parties. This began to change in the first two decades of the twentieth century, however, and Gompers was largely responsible. The new attitude marked a break from Gompers's ideas of a strict separation between trade unionism and politics; he came to believe that an alliance between labor unions and a political party could have distinct advantages for union members.

The turning point came during the presidential election of 1908, in which Republican William Howard Taft (1857–1930) ran against Democrat William Jennings Bryan (1860–1925), from Nebraska. Bryan, a fiery orator, was running for the third time and represented the interests of small farmers and working people against what he denounced as bankers and wealthy industrialists. For the first time, the AFL wholeheartedly plunged into the election on the side of the Democrat, Bryan. Issues in the election included imposing an income tax, enforcing an eight-hour maximum work day, and

In the 1908 presidential election, Samuel Gompers gave the support of the American Federation of Labor to William Jennings Bryan (pictured), marking the beginning of a long alignment between trade unions and the Democratic Party. *Reproduced by permission of the Library of Congress.*

setting in place government rules governing the operation of railroads and public utilities.

The Democrats lost the election of 1908, but the alignment of the AFL and the Democrats has continued. Woodrow Wilson (1856–1924), a Democrat, was elected president in 1912 and again in 1916 with the direct assistance of Gompers and the AFL.

World War I

America's entry into World War I (1914–18) in 1917 posed another crisis for Gompers. Traditionally, socialists opposed war, seeing it as a quarrel between the property-owning classes in which working people had no real interest. Now, President Wilson appealed for union support as the United States entered the fray on the side of Britain and France and against Germany and Austria. Gompers went along.

Gompers organized the War Committee on Labor and strongly opposed pacifism (opposition on moral grounds to war under any circumstances). During the Versailles peace conference held from 1919 to 1920 to settle the war, Gompers was named by President Wilson to serve on the Commission on International Labor Legislation. Wilson strongly advocated establishing new international rules to avoid future conflicts, most notably the establishment of the League of Nations, a precursor to the United Nations.

By that time, the alliance between Gompers and Wilson had become a strong, two-way affair. Wilson addressed the AFL convention in 1917, and the Labor Department under Wilson was aggressive in pushing the case of unions. Pro-labor laws such as the Clayton Antitrust Act and the Adamson Act passed Congress, and Gompers was named to the Council of National Defense.

In exchange for AFL support, Wilson backed important items on the union's agenda, such as shorter hours and higher pay. At the time, there was another union organization, the Industrial Workers of the World (IWW), that took a much more radical approach to improving the lives of workers. The IWW strongly backed class warfare pitting workers against owners, and viewed the government as the chief protector of business interests against the interests of workers. When the government tried to suppress members of the IWW, Gompers agreed with the action. It was the start of a decades-long alliance between trade union leaders and politicians who opposed radical measures to advance the interests of workers.

Labor unions had emerged from the dim shadows of socialism to the broad daylight of electoral politics.

Gompers continued battling for the cause of trade unionism right up to his death, at the age of seventy-four, in 1924. After he died, both business and labor leaders mourned his passing. He was recognized for having directed organized labor away from socialism and toward a cooperative relationship with employers.

For More Information

Books

Gompers, Samuel. *Seventy Years of Life and Labor: An Autobiography.* New York: A. M. Kelley, 1967.

Kaufman, Stuart Bruce. *Samuel Gompers and the Origins of the American Federation of Labor, 1848–1896.* Westport, CT: Greenwood Press, 1973.

Livesay, Harold C. *Samuel Gompers and Organized Labor in America.* Boston, MA: Little Brown. 1978.

Stearn, Gerald Emanuel. *Gompers.* Englewood Cliffs, NJ: Prentice-Hall, 1971.

Periodicals

Raskin, A. H. "Labor Enters a New Century." *New Leader,* November 30, 1981, p. 9.

Salvatore, Nick. "Talkin' Union: Gompers Among the Scholars." *New York Times Book Review,* August 31, 1986, p. 1.

Web Sites

"Samuel Gompers." *Earliest Voices: A Gallery from the Vincent Voice Library.* http://www.historicalvoices.org/earliest_voices/gompers.html#recordings (accessed on February 13, 2003).

"Testimony of Samuel Gompers (1883)." *History of the American Working Class.* http://www.uwm.edu/Course/448-440/gompers.htm (accessed on February 13, 2003).

Yellowitz, Irwin. "Samuel Gompers: A Half Century in Labor's Front Rank." *U.S. Bureau of Labor Statistics.* http://www.bls.gov/opub/mlr/1989/07/art4abs.htm (accessed on February 13, 2003).

Jay Gould

Born May 27, 1836
Roxbury, New York

Died December 2, 1892
New York, New York

American financier

"I can hire one-half the working class to kill the other half."

Jay Gould earned his fortune by means of financial manipulation, using investments in western U.S. railroads to gain a virtual monopoly on rail traffic to the southwestern quarter of the United States, giving him almost exclusive control over the rails in this region. He was one of the Industrial Revolution's so-called robber barons—owners of businesses that stifled competition in industries while amassing enormous fortunes. His business tactics and unethical behavior in pursuit of wealth made him widely disliked, both personally and professionally. But Gould's fortune did not survive even one generation. His son George took over the business upon Jay Gould's death and, through an overly ambitious expansion plan, lost control of all the railroads by 1918.

The story of U.S. railroads includes a long list of rogues, people who are dishonest or mischievous, who made their fortunes through secret and unfair business dealings. Jay Gould's name has long been at the top of this list, along with his business partner Jim Fisk (1834–1872), among others. Gould earned his reputation as a rogue partly because he was a financier, meaning that he made money by buying and sell-

Reproduced by permission of Getty Images.

ing the inventions and property of others, not an inventor himself. Gould's purpose was limited to making money, rather than contributing to the practical achievements of the Industrial Revolution, a period of fast-paced economic change that began in Great Britain in the middle of the eighteenth century.

Starting out

Unlike his contemporary, the master financier **J. P. Morgan** (1837–1913; see entry), Jay Gould did not start out as a wealthy young man. To the contrary, his origins were modest. His father, Jason Gould, owned a farm and a small store in Roxbury, New York, in the Catskill Mountains, northwest of New York City. His son, Jason Jr. (sometimes spelled Jayson), called Jay, was an intelligent and strong-willed boy who was driven to succeed.

While attending school, Gould worked in his father's store. In his spare time, he learned math and also how to survey land. At age sixteen, he started his own land-surveying business, and by the time he was twenty Gould used the money he had saved to go into partnership with an experienced tanner (someone who converts animal hide, or skin, into leather) in eastern Pennsylvania. He brought in a New York leather merchant, C. M. Leupp, as a third partner. But not long after, Leupp killed himself—Gould's enemies blamed Gould and what they considered his dishonest business practices for the suicide—and Gould moved to New York City, where he began dealing in the financial markets.

Playing the stock market

In 1860 Gould opened a brokerage house, a business where owners of stocks can buy and sell their shares, on the eve of the U.S. Civil War (1861–65). Initially, he concentrated on gold and government bonds. (Bonds are a form of government or corporate IOUs in which the issuer promises to pay a fixed amount sometime in the future; buyers pay an amount less than the "face amount." For example, the government might sell a one hundred dollar bond for $90, with the promise of redeeming the bond for $100 in a few years. The difference, $10 in this example, is the effective interest paid on the face amount of the bond.)

As train transportation grew rapidly in the United States, large cities constructed ornate and elaborate terminals, such as Grand Central Station in New York City (pictured). *Reproduced by permission of Getty Images.*

Later, Gould focused his attention on railroad stocks. It was the era when the Industrial Revolution was getting into full swing. In particular, many small companies were being created with the purpose of building railroads to haul raw materials (iron ore or coal, for example) from a mining site to manufacturing towns or to waterways. Trains also were used as passenger transportation in the rapidly growing United States. Building a railroad required a large investment at the start, which was raised by selling shares in the company and using the cash to lay the track and buy locomotives and railroad cars. Railroad shares in the middle of the nineteenth century were somewhat similar to shares in high-technology companies during the 1990s in that buying and selling the shares became a business in and of itself.

While Gould had launched a career that led to a reputation as a slick dealer, his personal life was another story. In 1863 he married a woman named Helen Day Miller and eventually had six children. He was, by all accounts, a dedicated

The Erie War, 1867–68

The railroad business in the 1800s had two aspects: 1) raising money to lay down tracks and establish a connection between two points (typically two cities); and 2) acquiring railroad companies, which usually owned the tracks between just two points, in order to build a network of rails and control the business of hauling freight over a wide region.

The Erie Railroad, by means of which Gould got a serious start in the business, is one example. The railroad originated in 1832 to connect the Hudson River with Lake Erie, creating an overland link between the Atlantic Ocean and the Great Lakes. Its western end was at Dunkirk, New York, southwest of Buffalo; it linked to the Hudson River at Piermont, New York, north of New York City.

Cornelius Vanderbilt's New York Central Railroad also linked these two points, via a different route, and Vanderbilt had an interest in dominating rail transport in the region.

Gould agreed to sell shares in the Erie to Vanderbilt, then proceeded to issue fifty thousand more shares of Erie stock, effectively diluting Vanderbilt's share of the company. A judge, possibly influenced by Vanderbilt's political friends, issued an order for Gould's arrest for violating a court order barring issuing of the shares, and Gould fled to nearby New Jersey. Gould made his way to the state capital in Albany,

family man who preferred spending time with his children to any other pursuit.

A dim reputation

It did not take long for Gould to earn a reputation as untrustworthy. The reputations of Gould and his business partner, Jim Fisk, for unethical business practices began, in particular, in a financial battle over the Erie Railroad Company. The story became known as "the Erie War" and took place between 1867 and 1868 (see box above).

Gould and Fisk, joined by a third partner, Daniel Drew (1788–1879), bought enough shares of the Erie Railroad on the stock exchange so that they were able to control the firm. Another pioneer in railroading, Cornelius Vanderbilt

New York, and (it is alleged) bribed legislators to legalize his action after the fact.

It was part of a two-year battle with Vanderbilt over control of the Erie, and plans to extend the railroad westward to Chicago. Both men were intent on controlling a monopoly on rail traffic between the nation's two largest cities and business centers. In the case of Jay Gould, double-dealing and financial manipulation were tools he used to meet his goal.

Eventually Gould paid Vanderbilt $1 million to end their struggle, and Gould kept control of the Erie. He expanded the railroad westward to Chicago, accumulating a large corporate debt in the process. Gould continued to engage in questionable financial stock dealings (similar to today's "insider trading," in which owners or employees buy and sell stock based on information not known to others). Eventually, the company was forced into bankruptcy in 1875, but not before Gould had made a fortune.

The fact that Jay Gould got rich from a company that itself was bankrupt helps explain why his reputation suffered, both during his lifetime and long afterward. Other pioneers of the Industrial Revolution made fortunes from companies that, in some cases, are still in business. Others, like Gould, seemed to drive companies into the ground as a means of getting rich.

(1794–1877), owned the New York Central Railroad, which like the Erie also operated in New York State. Vanderbilt wanted to buy the Erie as a means of gaining control of railroad transportation over a broader area, and of eliminating a potential competitor for the lucrative business of hauling freight and passengers between New York City and Chicago.

Gould, gold, and the panic of 1869

As part of his plans to acquire wealth through railroads, Gould controlled the Wabash, a railroad linking Toledo, Ohio, in the east to Chicago, Illinois; St. Louis, Missouri; and Omaha, Nebraska (with branches to Detroit, Michigan, and Buffalo, New York) in the west. It was a major transportation link in the wheat-growing area of the Midwest.

In the summer of 1869, Gould hatched a complex financial scheme that he hoped would encourage more wheat sales to Europe—and thus, more wheat shipments on his railroad. Gould's plan involved buying significant quantities of gold in order to drive up its price. Initially, his scheme worked, and the price of gold rose from $135 per ounce to $160. Then, on September 24, 1869, the government suddenly started selling gold from its large stocks. Within three hours, the price plunged back down to $135. People who had borrowed money to buy gold at higher prices, thinking it would continue rising, were in a panic to cash in and started selling their gold. Other investors sold shares in companies to raise cash, and stock prices also plunged.

Many investors, including Gould, lost money that day. Eventually the collapse of stock prices led to a slowdown in business—what's known as a recession in modern terms. Gould was widely blamed for trying to manipulate the price of gold and wheat, and for the resulting "panic."

Railroading and telegraphy

Gould's effort to manipulate the price of the Wabash Railroad failed, but that did not drive him out of the railroad business. In 1873, when an economic downturn drove down stock prices, Gould bought enough shares of the Texas and Pacific Railroad and the Missouri Pacific to control them. He also acquired stocks in smaller companies whose tracks linked into the Missouri Pacific and the Union Pacific (a third railroad in which Gould also owned shares). When the stock market recovered toward the end of the 1870s, Gould was in a position to reap huge profits from the railroads he owned and controlled. (Often, when a shareholder owns a substantial part of a company, though not necessarily more than half the shares, that shareholder is able to control the company's actions since there is no other block of shares large enough to vote down proposals made by the major stockholder. Control can mean both the operations of the company, and also policies regarding sharing of profits, paying dividends, and acquiring assets, such as another railroad or more land for new tracks.)

In the early 1880s Gould concentrated his attention on the Missouri Pacific, becoming more involved with running the business than with merely trading its stock. He bought minor railroad lines that fed into the Missouri Pacific and turned it into a major economic force. He invested about $50 million in the company (equivalent to about $900 million in 2002 prices), drove down the cost of shipping freight (threatening the business of his competitors), and acquired other railroads to expand his network.

Railroads were not the only industries in which Gould was active. He created a monopoly of elevated trains in New York City, the centerpiece of today's New York mass transit system.

Gould also started buying telegraph companies, starting with the American Union Telegraph in 1879 and including Western Union in 1881 and the telegraph system owned by the Baltimore and Ohio Railroad a few years later. At the end of the 1880s Gould's consolidated companies dominated the national telegraph industry, which played a critical role in rapid communications for newspapers and railroads.

Early death

In the winter of 1892 Gould contracted pneumonia, a lung disease caused by an infection that is often fatal if not treated with antibiotics, which were unavailable at that time. Gould died on December 2, 1892, at the relatively young age of fifty-six. His estate was valued at $77 million (worth about $1.5 billion in 2002 dollars). Unlike some of his contemporaries, such as **Andrew Carnegie** (1835–1919) and **John D. Rockefeller** (1839–1937; see entries), Gould did not distribute his wealth to charitable causes, perhaps in part because his death came unexpectedly at an age when he was still concentrating on building a bigger fortune.

Instead, Gould's estate went to his children, and in his will he handed control of the management of his ongoing properties to his son, George Jay Gould (1864–1923).

George Jay Gould

The story of George Jay Gould is in some respects the opposite of his father's. Whereas Jay Gould had used a variety of tactics in the stock market to build a railroad empire, Gould's son, George, also called Jay, fell victim to business tactics that eventually led to the loss of all the railroad properties acquired by his father. In rough terms, the father spent thirty years building up an empire; the son spent thirty years watching it disappear.

A privileged youth

Unlike his father, George Gould grew up in highly privileged circumstances. He attended a private school, then entered his father's business rather than attend college. This did not stop George from becoming an avid sportsman, engaging in many pastimes that mark the wealthy. Although George, like his father, was not a large man, he enjoyed boxing, fencing, hunting, yachting, and tennis. In particular he loved the game of polo, which is a bit like soccer, except that players are equipped with mallets and chase the ball on horseback. He owned his own polo field, plus a string of ponies. George enjoyed hunting and fishing on his estate in North Carolina, and he owned a lodge in the Berkshire Mountains of western Massachusetts. He was active in the theater and helped finance new plays. His main country home, in Lakewood, New Jersey, was said at the time to be one of the most magnificent private homes in the country.

The inheritance

George Jay Gould worked for his father's growing network of railroads until he was twenty-eight, when his father died unexpectedly after falling ill. George inherited almost complete control of his father's complex business empire, which included several railroads in the American West as well as elevated trains in New York City and various other enterprises.

Although inheriting a fortune is usually a strong advantage in life, it is not without its complications. In George Gould's case, his father's network of railroads was one of several competing for dominance and control of the lucrative business of shipping freight from California to the East Coast and vice versa.

Besides owning the Manhattan Elevated Railroad in New York City and Western Union, the country's leading telegraph company (soon to lose business to Alexander Graham Bell's [1847–1922] telephone), the Gould fortune was based on four railroads: the Missouri Pacific, the Texas and Pacific, the International and Great Northern, and the Wabash.

George Gould's strategic vision for these companies was to establish a railroad network that ran ocean to ocean. Gould was not the only railroad owner with this vision, however, and to achieve it he needed to start expanding. The Wabash, one of his principal holdings, ended at Buffalo, New York, for example, and could not carry freight all the way to ports on the Atlantic. Andrew Carnegie, the owner of the largest steel manufacturing company at the time, encouraged Gould to compete with the Pennsylvania Railroad, the only rail that was currently servicing Carnegie's Pittsburgh steel company. Gould invested in a new route that led from Toledo, Ohio, to Baltimore, Maryland, traveling through Pittsburgh. The project resulted in intense competition with the Pennsylvania Railroad, which, to get back at Gould for taking its business, ripped down the telegraph poles of Gould's Western Union.

Growing too fast

At the same time, Gould had a similar problem in the West: his railroad, the Missouri Pacific, did not actually extend to the Pacific. At one stage, his father had owned the Union Pacific, which did go all the way to the coast, but it had gone bankrupt in 1893 (not unlike other Gould properties that were essentially looted by the older Gould and then abandoned). An unrelated business quarrel with the Union Pacific's subsequent owner, Edward Harriman (1848–1909), resulted in all-out competition between the Union Pacific and Missouri Pacific. In this battle for business, George Gould was at a disadvantage because his railroad did not stretch as far west as did the Union Pacific.

Gould bought the Denver and Rio Grande Railroad in 1900, which extended his line to Salt Lake City, Utah, where the Union Pacific also ended. In turn, Harriman in 1901 bought the Southern Pacific, which enabled him to compete with Gould's properties for freight headed both north and south. Gould's response was to charter the Western Pacific Railroad and begin building tracks all the way to San Francisco, California.

At last, George Gould had a transcontinental route that ran from Baltimore on the Atlantic to San Francisco on the Pacific, challenging Harriman's monopoly based on the Pennsylvania Railroad.

But Gould's time was running out. The financial toll from nearly ten years of building a railroad through Pittsburgh (to serve the Carnegie steel interests) and across California's Sierra Nevada mountain range was enormous. And in the meantime the Panama Canal had opened, enabling ships to haul transcontinental freight that previously had to be transported by rail. Another precipitous drop in stock prices in 1907 further weakened Gould's financial position.

In addition, his competitors were buying up smaller regional railroads, which meant these companies were no longer directing their transcontinental freight business to Gould, but rather to Harriman's competing lines.

Weakened by fallen stock prices, Gould soon was unable to compete effectively against Harriman, who had strong financial allies. Several of his railroads went bankrupt, meaning they could not pay their debts and were ordered by the courts to be sold. George Jay Gould's railroad empire started shrinking; in 1912, he lost financial control of most of the railroads he once owned. Six years later, in 1918, the last Gould property, the Denver and Rio Grande, went bankrupt.

A life falling apart

Competition was not the only problem facing George Gould. He was constantly being dragged into court. In 1916 members of his own family brought suit against him, wanting a full accounting of what George had done with his father's estate. Three years later, in 1919, the court removed George Gould as the chief executor and trustee of the estate, on grounds that he had mixed his personal money with the riches that were part of his father's estate and intended to be shared with other siblings. The suit dragged on for another eight years, until 1927. It was reputed to be the most expensive lawsuit of its time over the disposition of an inheritance.

George had problems in his personal life as well. In 1886 he married Edith Kingdon, with whom he had seven children. In 1913 he began an affair with an actress named

Guinevere Jeanne Sinclair, with whom he had three children. George Gould acknowledged that he was the father of these children, and he married their mother in 1922, after his first wife died. About a year after their wedding, during a trip to France, George Gould came down with pneumonia and, like his father, died from the disease on May 16, 1923.

For More Information

Books

Hoyt, Edwin P. *The Goulds: A Social History.* New York: Weybright and Talley, 1969.

Klein, Maury. *The Life and Legend of Jay Gould.* Baltimore, MD: Johns Hopkins University Press, 1986.

Minnigerode, Meade. *Certain Rich Men: Stephen Girard, John Jacob Astor, Jay Cooke, Daniel Drew, Cornelius Vanderbilt, Jay Gould, Jim Fisk.* Freeport, NY: Books for Libraries Press, 1970.

Periodicals

Howard, Nat. "Fool's Gold." *D & B Reports,* July-August 1993, p. 46.

Lubar, Robert. "The Life and Legend of Jay Gould." *Fortune,* August 18, 1986, p. 96.

Web Sites

"Erie Railroad." *Western New York Railroad Archive.* http://wnyrails.railfan.net/erie_home.htm (accessed on February 10, 2003).

"Jay Gould Profile." *HarpWeek Biography.* http://elections.harpweek.com/2biographies/bio-1884-Full.asp?UniqueID=6&Year=1884 (accessed on February 10, 2003).

Troesken, Werner. "Monopolies in America: Empire Builders and Their Enemies from Jay Gould to Bill Gates." *Economic History Services.* http://www.eh.net/bookreviews/library/0280.shtml (accessed on February 13, 2003).

James J. Hill

Born September 16, 1838
Rockwood, Ontario, Canada

Died May 29, 1916
St. Paul, Minnesota

Canadian-born American railroad magnate

"The wealth of the country, its capital, its credit, must be saved from the predatory poor as well as the predatory rich, but above all from the predatory politician."

Reproduced by permission of Getty Images.

James J. Hill was a Canadian-born visionary who built not only a railroad linking the upper Midwest of the United States with the Pacific Ocean, but he helped populate the region with farmers recruited from Scandinavia. His career encompassed the whole range of events that comprised the Industrial Revolution, a period marked by the widespread replacement of manual labor by machines that began in Great Britain in the middle of the eighteenth century, including technology, population shifts, and political struggle. Although he was one of the most successful railroad builders of his era, Hill tangled with President **Theodore Roosevelt** (1858–1919; see entry) over the issue of his railroad monopoly—and lost.

As a railroader, Hill was highly successful. He insisted on using quality materials and careful surveys to build the most efficient routes possible. He combined his engineering know-how with the understanding that railroads serve customers, not merely places, and so he built a population base of immigrant farmers to go along with his railroads. His companies were often financially successful even as other railroads were declaring bankruptcy.

Hill was a tough business competitor. He managed to gain control over railroad transportation in the United States linking upper Midwestern farms and eastern factories with ocean ports on the West Coast, enabling him to dictate the cost of shipping farm produce to market and manufactured goods to farmers. It was this monopoly, or exclusive control of the regional industry, that brought him into direct conflict with President Roosevelt.

Despite his success in building a business in what was still considered the American wilderness, Hill's reputation in the end was linked to his losing legal battle with Roosevelt, which ended Hill's monopoly. Hill's was the first trust (a group of companies acquired by a single owner intent on discouraging competition in an industry) that Roosevelt, "the Trust Buster," busted.

Birth and childhood

James Jerome Hill was born in Canada, in the small town of Rockwood, Ontario, in 1838. He was the descendant of a Scottish family that had immigrated to British North America. He was the fifth son named James, and decided later in life to give himself a middle name to distinguish himself. Legend has it that he wanted to name himself after Napoléon Bonaparte (1769–1821), the French emperor, but decided that would seem too self-important and instead settled on the name of Napoléon's brother, Jerome.

Hill's father died when Hill was young, forcing him to drop out of school to help support his family. As a boy, he lost sight in one eye as a result of an accident with a bow and arrow.

During the summer before his eighteenth birthday, Hill took a steamboat to the town of St. Paul, Minnesota. St. Paul is on the Mississippi River, at the northernmost point where it is navigable. It was a popular gathering point in 1856 for fur trappers launching their annual treks. It was Hill's plan to become a fur trapper himself, but he arrived just a few days after the last group of trappers had left for the year, meaning that he would have to wait a year for his next chance.

In the meantime, Hill got a job working for the Mississippi River Steamboat Company as a shipping agent. It was a fateful choice since it placed Hill at the center of the freight business—a business he was destined to transform.

Although he was Canadian, Hill tried to enlist in the Union Army (that of the Northern states) during the U.S. Civil War (1861–65), but he was rejected because of his partial blindness. Instead, he spent the war years learning about the freight business. In 1866 Hill became an agent (local representative) for the St. Paul and Pacific Railroad. While working as an agent, Hill concluded that coal was a more efficient fuel than wood to power steam engines, and he formed a business to supply the railroad with coal—on an exclusive basis.

Always eager for new business opportunities, in 1872 Hill and a fellow Scot, Norman Kittson, organized a steamship company that operated on the north-flowing Red River, linking St. Paul, Minnesota, to Fort Garry, Manitoba (which is now the city of Winnipeg). Hill thought the land north of St. Paul would be good for agriculture, and that there was a good business opportunity in extending a railroad line north to Fort Garry. From Kittson, Hill learned the techniques of defeating the competition by reducing rates and even, on one occasion, ramming a competitor's steamboat

The era of the railroads

Hill had launched his steamboat business just as trains were on the verge of replacing riverboats as the principal means of long-distance travel and shipment of goods in the United States. The years following the U.S. Civil War saw a boom in railroad building all over the United States. In 1862 the Pacific Railway Act had granted a handful of railroad companies huge tracts of land to extend railroads to the Pacific. With the end of the war, railroad construction picked up steam, resulting in the "golden spike" driven at Promontory, Utah, on May 10, 1869, marking the completion of the first rail line to cross the country.

At the same time, streams of European immigrants were flocking to the United States in search of inexpensive land and new opportunities. This mass migration of Europeans was largely the result of a three-way cooperation between the U.S. government, the railroads, and the immigrants. For the most part, the states of the U.S. West were occupied only by native Americans in the years just after the Civil War. The federal government claimed title to vast stretches of territory and was eager to populate the country with Europeans to solidify control of the continent for the United States government. To accomplish its goal, the government turned over ownership of millions of acres to companies willing to finance the construction of railroads. In turn, these companies were able to sell this land at very low prices to settlers from Europe who wanted to own their own farms. These sales not only served as a source of cash to build the railroads, they also created a business opportunity. The railroads would have customers to ship grain and other agricultural goods to the cities in the East as well as potential customers for manufactured goods in the newly settled West.

One of those building on this proposition was Jay Cooke, a banker who received forty-seven million acres of land in the Northwest United States to help build the Northern Pacific Railroad. But in 1873, in the midst of trying to raise $100 million to complete the line, his firm went bankrupt. The failure of Cooke's well-known and well-respected firm resulted in a panic on the New York Stock Exchange, which was forced to close for ten days. Subsequently, the financial panic resulted in the failure of thousands of other businesses, including the St. Paul and Pacific Railroad, Hill's old employer and customer for coal.

Empire builder of the Northwest

The national financial crisis in 1873 gave Hill his chance. When the stock market plunge and failure of the St. Paul and Pacific Railroad suddenly put the company on the market, Hill found three partners, including the Bank of Montreal, and bought the St. Paul and Pacific for $280,000 (about $4.2 million in 2002 prices). Hill thought the financial panic had reduced the price of the railroad to about one-fifth of its value. It was not the last time that Hill took advantage of a crisis in the U.S. financial markets to expand his business empire.

Among the four partners, Hill was the most knowledgeable about the railroad business, and he set about extending the line and making it profitable. Hill's companies received from the federal government two million acres of land

The New York Stock Exchange. When the stock market plunged in 1873, James J. Hill took the opportunity to purchase the St. Paul and Pacific Railroad company at a reduced price. *Reproduced by permission of the Corbis Corporation.*

in Minnesota in exchange for extending the railroad to connect with the Canadian Pacific Railroad at St. Vincent, Minnesota. The year was 1879. The completion of the link coincided with two years of successful harvests, which resulted in more business for the railroad. The abundant crops also attracted immigrants from Norway and Sweden, who were willing to pay between $2.50 and $5.00 an acre for family farms carved out of the land that was given to Hill and his partners.

Hill was a hands-on manager of his railroad. Not content simply to direct operations from afar, he often worked around the clock, examining the proposed route of tracks and attending to scores of details. He studied fields alongside his railroads, making sure the line was being built on the flattest tracts of land. If needed, Hill directed workers to move tons of earth to smooth out the land, knowing that this would pay off in the long run in saving fuel and enabling his trains to run faster.

Just a year after buying the St. Paul and Pacific, Hill launched plans to extend his railroad west to the Pacific Ocean, even though there were already three other competing railroads: the Union Pacific, Central Pacific, and Northern Pacific, all built with enormous grants of public land.

In 1886 Hill's railroad, the Great Northern, had reached Minot, North Dakota. While the competing Northern Pacific line, with tracks south of Hill's, ran through land unsuitable for agriculture, Hill engineered his railway through land that would support farmers who could become future customers, paying to ship their crops to the East. His construction techniques were superior, and he was careful to avoid steep hills that would slow trains and use more fuel. By October 1887 the tracks had reached Great Falls, Montana. Eight thousand men and thirty-three hundred teams of horses were employed in pushing the tracks westward.

A key business strategy of Hill's involved populating the territory that his railroad was serving. He gave immigrants a discount on rail travel if they promised to settle along the railroad's route. His representatives recruited tens of thousands of Europeans to take advantage of his offer; in the process, these immigrants became future customers of Hill's railroad. It was Hill's conviction that he was building a railroad to serve people, not places, and that it was in his interests to bring in people along with the railroad. Hill and his agents traveled to Europe, especially Scandinavian countries, to encourage people to immigrate to the United States and buy farms near his railroad. It was a business philosophy unique in the golden age of railroads.

Hill sold lumber at low cost along his routes to help encourage the building of new towns. He imported cattle and gave away cows to farmers, also to encourage economic growth.

In some respects Hill was wildly successful. In Montana, for example, more than six million acres were settled in a period of just two years. (Later, however, drought—very little to no rainfall for extended periods of time— and the deep plowing of the land that resulted from the settlement caused severe soil erosion in Montana and the Dakotas. As a result, wheat production plunged by 90 percent between 1916 and 1919. Many farmers originally encouraged by Hill to settle in this part of the United States were forced off the land as a result.)

Hill was always eager to build business for his railroad and to expand his holdings in areas where businesses needed railroad transportation. He dispatched agents to Asia to study its imports and exports, looking for goods he could ship across North America in the era before the Panama Canal allowed ships access from the Pacific to U.S. ports on the Atlantic. Similarly he searched New England and the southern states looking for goods that could be shipped by rail to the Pacific for transport to Asia.

In 1893, Hill's railroad reached the Pacific, at Everett, Washington, providing the port city of Seattle with a much-needed rail link to the East Coast.

The panic of 1893

Another nationwide financial panic in 1893 forced most of the giant transcontinental railroads into bankruptcy, including Hill's most obvious competitor, the Northern Pacific. Hill's railroad, on the other hand, survived the economic slowdown that resulted. To stay in business, Hill fired a thousand workers and slashed the pay of those who kept their jobs. He became the target of bitterness and hatred from these workers, who blamed him for their economic woes in an era that knew nothing of unemployment insurance and government assistance.

As in 1873, Hill moved quickly to profit from the situation by taking control of the Northern Pacific, again with help from the Bank of Montreal. When the attorney general of Minnesota objected—on the basis of a Minnesota law banning the merger of parallel, competing railroads—Hill entered into an alliance with the New York financier **J. P. Morgan** (1837–1913; see entry). Morgan acquired and reorganized the

Northern Pacific, then entered into a business alliance, in 1896, with the Great Northern, the Northern Pacific's chief competitor. Under terms of the deal, the companies formed "a permanent alliance, defensive, and in case of need offensive, with a view of avoiding competition."

Practically speaking, the two companies operated as one. The arrangement was a prototype (working example) of the sort of monopolistic practices carried out in many industries in the 1890s. The deal gave Hill control over shipping to points all across the northern tier of the United States. He could dictate freight rates to farmers, lumber companies, and manufacturers wanting to ship their goods to market, or to bring in raw materials.

Hill was also bent on acquiring the Chicago, Burlington and Quincy railroad line in order to have a link between the Great Lakes and the Rocky Mountains. With J. P. Morgan, Hill arranged to buy the line, beating out another railroad tycoon, Edward H. Harriman (1848–1909), head of the Union Pacific, who also had wanted the route.

A trust, busted

Not easily defeated in his quest to dominate railroad traffic to the West Coast, Harriman determined to get his revenge by quietly buying shares in Hill's main firm, the Northern Pacific Railroad, in order to wrest it away from Hill and Morgan (who were the largest stockholders, but who did not own all the shares). Harriman's purchases drove up the cost of stock in Northern Pacific, and Hill suspected what was happening. He rushed to New York to meet with Morgan and jointly start a bidding war for the shares in Northern Pacific that he did not already own.

In just three days, shares in the Northern Pacific soared from $114 to $1,000 as Hill and Harriman battled for control of the line by offering more and more money to stockholders willing to sell their shares. Soon, representatives of the two sides negotiated a truce and organized a new company called Northern Securities Company, which was designed to oversee the management of Hill's interests, including the Great Northern Railroad; the Northern Pacific; and the Chicago, Burlington and Quincy. Harriman was given a seat on the board of directors and shares in the new company, but Hill and Morgan had controlling interest.

To outsiders, the Northern Securities Company looked like a trust—a company that buys other firms in an industry in an effort to limit competition, in this case, the competition between the Northern Pacific and the Great Northern.

To Hill, the Northern Securities Company was a reasonable way of making railroad service more efficient by eliminating redundant (unnecessary doubling) resources. But to President Theodore Roosevelt, the company not only looked like a trust, but also looked like a violation of the 1890 Sherman Antitrust Act, which had outlawed companies designed to stifle competition. On February 20, 1902, it became the first—but far from the last—target of Roosevelt's trust-busting campaign designed to enforce the 1890 law. The federal government sued to break up the Northern Securities Company.

Morgan rushed to Washington to meet Roosevelt and try to head off the government's suit, offering to "fix it up" if he had done something wrong. But Roosevelt was not interested in negotiating with Morgan; he wanted to establish a new principle in dealing with trusts. The president felt an offer to "fix it up" would do little to discourage the practice by Morgan and others of buying up competing companies in order to control whole industries. It was a subject that worried Morgan, who had organized a similar trust for the steel industry by acquiring **Andrew Carnegie**'s (1835–1919; see entry) steel company. Hill, on the other hand, was convinced that competition was wasteful and prevented railroads from operating efficiently. He was sure he would win in court.

Hill found out differently a year later, in April 1903, when the U.S. Court of Appeals ruled against him and for the government. A year after that, the U.S. Supreme Court, in a 5-4 vote, upheld the appeals court ruling and insisted that the Northern Securities Company be broken up into its original companies—effectively returning to the situation that existed before Hill's bidding war with Harriman over the Northern Pacific.

One more battle

Hill fought one more battle with Harriman: for domination of railroad traffic in Oregon. Starting in 1905, Hill decided to begin laying track south from Washington State into Oregon. It was an area that Harriman considered his operating territory, since he owned Union Pacific and Southern Pacific, which served the state. Hill built a rail line along the Deschutes River through a sparsely populated part of the state. Harriman was convinced that Hill planned to lay track right on south to San Francisco, California, and was determined to stop him by laying track along the other side of the river. The two sides worked feverishly side by side. Eventually, both companies reached a narrow pass with room for only one set of tracks. Harriman managed to buy the right of way, stopping the competition—for a time. Later, Hill put steamships into service to ship freight from the coast of Oregon to San Francisco, in competition with Harriman's freight line.

End of the road

In 1907, at age sixty-nine, Hill went into semiretirement and appointed his son Louis to lead the Great Northern. In May 1916 Hill became ill with an infection that doctors could not control, and he died on May 29. At the time of his funeral two days later, all the trains on the Great Northern line came to a stop for five minutes in his honor.

For More Information

Books

Holbrook, Stewart H. *James J. Hill: A Great Life in Brief.* New York: Knopf, 1955.

Malone, Michael P. *James J. Hill: Empire Builder of the Northwest.* Norman, OK: University of Oklahoma Press, 1996.

Martin, Albro. *James J. Hill and the Opening of the Northwest.* Oxford, U.K., and New York: Oxford University Press, 1976.

Periodicals

Morse, Minna. "The First Empire Builder of the Northwest." *Smithsonian,* October 1999, p. 130.

Schutz, Howard. "Giants in Collision: The Northern Pacific Panic of 1901." *American History Illustrated,* September 1986, p. 28.

Web Sites

"James J. Hill." *University of Houston.* http://voteview.uh.edu/jjhill.htm (accessed on February 13, 2003).

Muller, Christopher. "James J. Hill." *Rail Serve: The Internet Railroad Directory.* http://www.railserve.com/JJHill.html (accessed on February 13, 2003).

Mary Harris Jones (Mother Jones)

Born May 1, 1830
County Cork, Ireland

Died November 30, 1930
Silver Spring, Maryland

Irish-born American labor organizer

Once a teacher and dressmaker, Mary Harris Jones, otherwise known as Mother Jones, became a legendary labor organizer and champion of workers' rights. At a time when women were denied a role in politics, Jones played an active part in helping to correct the excesses of the Industrial Revolution, a period marked by the widespread replacement of manual labor by machines that began in Great Britain in the middle of the eighteenth century.

In the U.S. Senate, she was denounced as the "grandmother of all agitators" (someone who stirs up public feeling on controversial issues). Among poor workers, she was fondly called "Mother Jones." People who saw her stand up to speak at union gatherings were at first taken in by her kindly, demure (modest) look. But there was nothing at all demure about what Jones had to say, and she did not shrink from saying it loudly, in strong, plain words. Jones's calling was speaking out for the rights and dignity of workers, and in this she never tired.

The Industrial Revolution eventually resulted in an enormous improvement in the everyday lives of workers

"I live in the United States, but I do not know exactly where. My address is wherever there is a fight against oppression.... My address is like my shoes: it travels with me.... I abide where there is a fight against wrong."

Reproduced by permission of the Library of Congress.

worldwide, none more so than in the United States. But along the way, workers of all ages, from children of six to adults of sixty, sometimes suffered cruelly from hunger, from disease, from living in tumbledown shacks or overcrowded city slums (poor, rundown neighborhoods). Death or crippling injuries caused by industrial accidents were common. Jones spent her entire life—into her one-hundredth year—leading a struggle to improve the lives of working people in the United States. In *The Autobiography of Mother Jones,* she agreed with the description of her voiced in the Senate, that she was an agitator: "I'm not a humanitarian," she said. "I'm a hell-raiser."

As Mother Jones, the life of Mary Harris Jones took on a larger-than-life, almost mythical, quality. Much of what we know of her early years comes from her own autobiography, written late in her life. She did not become a full-time labor organizer until she was in her sixties, when she turned into a powerful symbol for the union movement: a grandmotherly figure behind whose modest appearance was a determination to fight against the social injustices of the Industrial Revolution.

Born in Ireland to a family of rebels

Mary Harris was the oldest child of poor tenant farmers who tried to scratch out a living on a scraggly piece of rented land in Cork, Ireland. The land and any crops on it belonged to a British landlord, as was common in those days. There was no such thing as a tenant farmer making a profit; profits, if any, went to the landlord, who might sometimes toss a bit of money to his tenants. In addition, tenants owed money for the rent of the land. When they couldn't pay the rent, which happened often, they were thrown off the land and out of their homes.

In the 1830s many of these poor, starving people were desperate enough to act against the landlords by burning and vandalizing property. British troops were called in to restore order. Mary Harris's grandfather was hanged for resisting the troops, and her father would have been hanged too, if the British had found him. He eluded authorities and eventually made it safely to the United States. Soon he was working on a construction crew in New York and saving his money to bring his family to America.

In 1838 Mary, her mother, and two younger brothers left Ireland and crossed the Atlantic Ocean to join her father. The family settled in Toronto, Canada, where they had enough money to live comfortably. Young Mary and her brothers all went to the public schools, where Mary did especially well. After elementary school, Mary went on to high school while her brothers left school to work for the railroad. Mary excelled at giving speeches and debating, and after graduation she went on to college, intending to become a teacher. From her mother she had learned how to make dresses, ensuring that she would have another marketable skill going out into the world.

In 1859 Mary was teaching at a Roman Catholic school in Detroit, Michigan. She became disheartened with the harsh rules and the low pay and decided to try dressmaking in Chicago, Illinois. "I preferred sewing to bossing little children," she wrote in her autobiography. But this job did not prove successful, so when she heard that there were teaching jobs in Memphis, Tennessee, in 1861, she decided to try her luck there. It was a turning point in her life.

Awakening the tiger

Within a few months of arriving in Memphis, Mary Harris met and married George Jones, a skilled ironworker. George was an active member of the Iron Molders International Union, which aimed to gain better working conditions and better pay for its members. She and her new husband were of the same mind about how to look at the world. For instance, they were both opposed to slavery; although in the pro-slave South during the U.S. Civil War (1861–65), they had to be careful about what they said.

Mary experienced for herself the poverty and slum conditions that were the lot of factory workers at that time. She and her family lived in the Pinch area of Memphis, where many working-class Irish immigrants lived in overcrowded, rundown, and unhealthy conditions. She experienced through her husband the nightmarish conditions in which he worked: twelve hours huddled over a workbench in a dark room where the fire was almost unbearably hot.

The U.S. Civil War ended in 1865, and for the next couple of years things were looking up for the Jones family.

They now had four young children. George was elected an official of the Iron Molders Union and traveled about spreading the union message and organizing workers. Mary eagerly supported her husband's union work.

It is unknown whether Mary had ever heard of yellow fever before the deadly infectious disease, which is spread by mosquitoes, struck her family in 1867. Within a week, her four children, ranging in age from a few weeks to five years, were dead. Her husband died that same year, in an industrial accident. At age thirty-seven, Mary was left alone. Her salvation was her ability to look outside of herself. Soon she was caring for other victims of yellow fever.

Back to Chicago

Mary Harris Jones had been devastated by the sudden death of her husband and children, but she realized that she had to go on living and decided to return to Chicago for another try at dressmaking. Her experiences as the wife of a union organizer and her work in Chicago made her increasingly aware of the marked contrast between the lifestyles of her wealthy clients and the workers just barely making a living in factories.

The Great Chicago Fire of 1871 devastated the city, including Mary Harris Jones's home and seamstress shop. *Reproduced by permission of AP/Wide World Photos.*

"We worked for the aristocrats of Chicago, and I had ample opportunity to observe the luxury and extravagance of their lives," Jones wrote in her autobiography. "Often while sewing for the lords and barons who lived in magnificence on the Lake Shore Drive, I would look out of the plate glass windows and see the poor, shivering wretches, jobless and hungry, walking along the frozen lake front. The contrast of their condition with that of the tropical comfort of the people for whom I sewed was painful to me. My employers seemed neither to notice nor to care."

Just as she was gaining financial success, disaster struck Jones a second time. The great Chicago fire of 1871 destroyed one-sixth of the city, including Jones's home, shop, and all her possessions. Once again, her response was to step forward and help others, organizing soup kitchens and finding shelter for those left homeless after the fire.

Taking shelter in a church basement after the Chicago fire, she happened on a meeting of the Knights of Labor, a labor union formed just two years earlier by garment workers in Philadelphia, Pennsylvania. The union's message of fighting for better pay and working conditions reawakened Jones's childhood experience of revolution in Ireland and her late husband's role as a labor union organizer. For the next half century, Jones traveled across the United States without a permanent home, promoting the causes of organized labor.

Mother Jones

By the 1880s, Jones had been working with a labor union for nearly ten years and had become known for her fiery speeches. She was able to lecture to prospective union members as if she were their mother, and the mine workers even called her "mother." Her age commanded respect, and her speaking skills held the workers' attention. Jones spoke the language of the streets, and her speeches were dotted with swear words. The rough and unskilled workers in the newly developing factories loved her style.

Where there was labor strife, Mother Jones was often there. Her rallying call in speeches to workers became famous: "Pray for the dead, and fight like hell for the living." In 1890 Mother Jones was hired as a paid organizer for the United Mine Workers Union (UMW). She also continued to campaign on behalf of textile workers, especially children (who often worked in factories during this time), as well as railroad workers.

The miners

Mother Jones spent much of her union career working on behalf of coal miners, especially in West Virginia and Colorado. Her role in these campaigns, which often involved violence, was a major contributor to her fame.

Starting with a miners' strike in Norton, Virginia, in 1891, Mother Jones took advantage of the sexism of her opponents in the battle with mine owners. She dressed conservatively, in long, lacy dresses and always in a bonnet. How could such a modest, elderly lady pose a threat in the rough, male world of coal mining? Yet violence often seemed to break out after her speeches. During a strike in Charleston, West Virginia, she urged miners' wives and children to protect themselves. How? "Buy every gun in Charleston," she advised.

She was not easily discouraged. Barred from crossing mine property or from renting meeting halls, she waded up streams to get to miners or held rallies on public roads. The terrain of West Virginia made organizing particularly difficult since miners often lived in isolated towns owned by the coal mining companies. But in that state alone, she participated in five major strikes over forty years.

Mother Jones also campaigned among coal miners in Colorado. In 1902 she led a strike by sixteen thousand coal miners throughout the state. But mine union leader John L. Lewis (1880–1969) decided to concentrate on another strike in eastern Pennsylvania, and called off the strike in Colorado. Mother Jones was furious. She denounced Lewis and left the United Mine Workers, staying away for the next nine years.

After Colorado, Mother Jones seemed to turn up everywhere. She supported striking machinists at the Southern Pacific Railroad. She supported copper miners in Arizona, and while there took on the cause of Mexican revolutionaries who had been imprisoned in the United States. On their behalf she met President William Howard Taft (1857–1930), after which a congressional committee was formed to investigate the matter.

In 1911 she rejoined the United Mine Workers and was again active in organizing miners in West Virginia. During a strike in 1912, she spoke out in a series of meetings. A military court accused her of conspiracy to commit murder after it was rumored that she planned to attack the governor during a march on the state capital. She was sentenced to twenty years in prison. (Her sentence was later set aside, but the incident was a measure of fear inspired in authorities by a woman who was by then eighty years old.)

Coffins of victims of the 1914 Ludlow (Colorado) massacre pass by a church. The incident incited a public furor over the anti-union tactics of mine owners. *Reproduced by permission of the Corbis Corporation.*

From 1913 to 1915, Mother Jones again led strikes in Colorado, at coal mines owned by **John D. Rockefeller** (1839–1937; see entry). State authorities tried every possible tactic to keep her away. She was ordered quarantined (removed from the general population so as not to spread disease) on the false grounds of having been exposed to smallpox. She was escorted out of Colorado by the state militia (now called the National Guard), but she sneaked back in and led a march of two thousand union delegates to the state capital. Arrested again in Trinidad, Colorado, she was held in a hospital for nine weeks, then in the cellar of a courthouse in Walsenburg, Colorado, where she threw bottles at rats that invaded her cell during the night.

In return for her support of Mexican revolutionaries a few years earlier, the Mexican revolutionary leader Pancho Villa (1878–1923) contacted President Woodrow Wilson (1856–1924) in an appeal for her release.

The Ludlow Massacre

During the Colorado miners' campaign, striking miners near Ludlow, Colorado, had been evicted from their company-owned homes and were living in tents. At ten o'clock on the morning of April 20, 1914, a combined force of state militiamen and private guards from the Baldwin Felts Detective Agency surrounded the large group of tents. Gunfire broke out—each side blamed the other for shooting first—between the guards, armed with a machinegun mounted on an armored car, and miners armed with rifles. Afterward, the private guards set fire to the tents, in the process suffocating some women and children who had crawled into pits for protection from the gunfire.

In the end, twenty people, including twelve women and children, were dead. The event came to be known as the Ludlow massacre, and the mine owner, John D. Rockefeller (1839-1937; see entry), was blamed by many labor leaders for murdering innocent people in order to defeat the union.

Nevertheless, the next year Mother Jones encountered Rockefeller in New York City and was invited to his office. Afterward, she said "I don't hold the boy responsible," which outraged many of her fellow radicals.

Children's crusade

The plight of children working in mines and factories had long been a central concern for Mother Jones. At the time, children as young as six were employed doing dangerous and unhealthy work, often for as long as sixteen hours a day, six days a week, for very low wages. The children of poor workers had no formal schooling, and there were few restrictions on how long they could be forced to work, or under what conditions.

In the summer of 1903, Mother Jones, at age seventy-three, led a march from Kensington, Pennsylvania, near Philadelphia, to Oyster Bay, New York, the home of President **Theodore Roosevelt** (1858–1919; see entry). The route was about 130 miles. She headed up an army of textile workers, half of them under sixteen, most of them dressed in rags and many with missing fingers as a result of injuries sustained from tiring, long days working at automated looms. They were a small fraction of the estimated two million children employed in factories, mines, and mills in the United States at the time. The labor agitator who looked like she could be the grandmother of the children marching with her was determined to confront President Roosevelt at his home in a campaign to establish child labor laws.

New York Senator Thomas Platt (1833–1910) was also on the marchers' list of people to see, but when he heard that Mother Jones was on her way, he reportedly dashed out the back door of his hotel and jumped onto a passing trolley. President Roosevelt told the Secret Service, whose job it was to guard the president, to keep the marchers away, but Mother Jones dressed three mill boys in fancy clothing and approached Roosevelt's house posed as ordinary tourists. The president turned them away from his door, saying he could do nothing.

Nevertheless, Mother Jones's march succeeded in drawing attention to the plight of children and raised a national outcry. Soon afterward, state legislatures began passing laws to protect children and to take steps to enforce laws that were already on the books.

Now she sleeps

Jones remained active in the labor cause right up until her death in 1930, although once she reached her nineties, age slowed her down significantly. In her last years, she lived with a friend in Silver Spring, Maryland, a suburb of Washington, D.C.

When she died, at the age of one hundred, Mother Jones was buried as she had asked: at the Miner's Cemetery in Mount Olive, Illinois, just northeast of St. Louis, Missouri. Her grave is next to those of miners who died in a mine riot in Virden, Illinois, in 1898. "I hope it will be my consolation when I pass away," she had said, in a document filed with the county government in 1924, "to feel I sleep under the clay with those brave boys."

In 1936 a granite monument was erected in the cemetery. A crowd of fifty thousand people attended a ceremony to honor the memory of Mother Jones. On her tombstone were carved the words: "She gave her life to the world of labor, her blessed soul to heaven. God's finger touches her, and now she sleeps."

Mother Jones was a powerful force in righting the wrongs of the Industrial Revolution and standing up for workers. Because of her lifelong struggle and fighting spirit, this "grandmother of agitators" has attained mythic status in the American historical consciousness.

For More Information

Books

Currie, Stephen. *We Have Marched Together: The Working Children's Crusade.* Minneapolis, MN: Lerner Publications Co., 1997.

Gorn, Elliott J. *Mother Jones: The Most Dangerous Woman in America.* New York: Hill and Wang, 2001.

Jones, Mary Harris. *The Autobiography of Mother Jones.* Chicago, IL: C. H. Kerr, 1972.

Whitman, Alden, ed. *American Reformers.* New York: H. W. Wilson Company, 1985.

Periodicals

Gorn, Elliott J. "Mother Jones: The Woman." *Mother Jones,* May 2001, p. 58.

Gustaitis, Joseph. "Mary Harris Jones: 'The Most Dangerous Woman in America.'" *American History Illustrated,* January 1988, p. 22.

Web Sites

Hawse, Mara Lou. "Mother Jones: The Miners's Angel." *Illinois Labor History Society.* http://www.kentlaw.edu/ilhs/majones.htm (accessed on February 13, 2003).

Jones, Mary Harris. "The Autobiography of Mother Jones." *MotherJones.com.* http://www.motherjones.com/about_us/MJbio.pdf (accessed on February 13, 2003).

Karl Marx

Born May 5, 1818
Trier, Germany

Died March 14, 1883
London, England

German political philosopher, writer

Karl Marx was a writer and political philosopher who responded to the rise of the working class with a theory of popular revolution that inspired generations of would-be revolutionaries in the industrialized world and beyond. He advocated the abolition of capitalism (private ownership of goods and services) and all private profit, by means of violence if necessary. Known as Marxism, his ideas inspired the famous Russian Revolution in 1917, and two of the world's largest countries, Russia and China, came to be governed by people who claimed to follow Marx's teaching.

Despite having many of his original ideas proved wrong, or distorted and misrepresented by governments claiming to be Marxist, Marx was one of the most influential writers and philosophers produced by the Industrial Revolution, a period marked by the widespread replacement of manual labor by machines that began in Great Britain in the middle of the eighteenth century. For better or for worse, his theories outlining how he thought communism would eventually triumph everywhere, inspired revolutionaries around the world for more than a century.

"The worker has become a commodity, and he is lucky if he can find a buyer. And the demand on which the worker's life depends is regulated by the whims of the wealthy and the capitalists."

Reproduced by permission of the Library of Congress.

Marx imagined that factory workers in Europe would rise up in revolt against their low pay and poor living conditions, and replace private ownership of factories with common ownership—communism. Few of Marx's predictions came about. In countries claiming the label "Marxist"—including the Soviet Union (now called the Russian Federation) and China—communism was imposed from the top by force, not by a popular uprising, and kept in power through means of harsh dictatorships. On the other hand, some of the outcomes Marx advocated—government control over the economy via elected parliaments—have come about, and his ideas strongly influenced countless politicians as well as revolutionaries.

Childhood and youth

Karl Marx was born in Trier, a town on the Moselle River in what was then called Prussia (now a part of Germany). His father, Heinrich Marx, was a prominent lawyer. Both his father and mother, Henriette Presburg Marx from Holland, were descendants of Jewish rabbis. But Heinrich Marx converted to Lutheranism the year before Karl was born in order to keep his job (Jews were barred from practicing law in Prussia at the time). Karl was baptized as a Christian when he was six years old and attended a Lutheran elementary school.

At age seventeen, Marx began studying law at the University of Bonn. He was not a serious student, and his main achievement in Bonn was meeting Jenny von Westphalen, whom he later married. After just one year in Bonn, Marx's father decided to send him to the University of Berlin, where he hoped his son would become more serious about school. The transfer worked, although perhaps not exactly in the way that the elder Marx had hoped.

At the University of Berlin, Marx became involved in a group called the Young Hegelians, named for their interest in the ideas of the German philosopher Georg Wilhelm Friedrich Hegel (pronounced GAY-org VIL-helm FREE-drick HAY-gull; 1770–1831). It was a significant association because later in life, Marx would adapt to his own theories a significant part of Hegel's ideas about how progress occurs in history. His association also brought Marx into contact with other student radicals who rejected the conventional way of viewing the world.

Marx spent four years studying the history of philosophy at the University of Berlin, and completed his studies in 1841. His clash with established authority began almost immediately. Marx had wanted to become a philosophy professor at the University of Bonn, but because of his radical views the conservative government of Prussia did not approve his appointment. Instead, Marx turned to journalism to earn a living. It was a fateful turn of events.

A radical editor and writer

In 1842 Marx became the editor of a newspaper called *Rheinische Zeitung* (Rhein Newspaper) in the city of Cologne, Germany. After about a year, the conservative (and antidemocratic) Prussian authorities forced it to close in order to stop it from publishing articles critical of the government.

Marx moved to Paris, France, where he became involved with the politics of the working class. There, he abandoned his goal of teaching philosophy and instead committed himself to changing the system of government.

After only two years, Marx was expelled from France, where his political activities and views annoyed and worried the authorities, and moved to Belgium for three years. In Brussels, Belgium, Marx helped found the German Workers' Party, and became active in a group named the Communist League, an organization of German workers who advocated a violent revolution to take over the government and seize private property. In 1847 the Communist League commissioned Marx and his friend Friedrich Engels (1820–1895) to write a statement of principals, which they called "The Manifesto of the Communist Party" (now generally called the *The Communist Manifesto*). It remains the most famous and widely quoted of Marx's works, especially its opening sentence: "A spectre is haunting Europe—the spectre of communism." (A spectre is a spirit that haunts or disturbs the mind.)

The same year that *The Communist Manifesto* was published, 1848, uprisings by workers broke out in several European countries, including France, although the manifesto did not play a large role in the unrest. (The primary cause of rioting was a prolonged economic slowdown that left many work-

The Writings of Karl Marx

Following is a list of the principal works of Karl Marx. Some were not published until after his death.

- *The Holy Family* (1845)
- *The Poverty of Philosophy* (1847)
- *The Communist Manifesto* (1848; with Friedrich Engels)
- *The Class Struggles in France* (1849)
- *The Eighteenth Brumaire of Louis Bonaparte* (1852)
- *The Critique of Political Economy* (1859)
- *Das Kapital* (Capital) (1867)*
- *The Civil War in France (1871)*

* Only the first volume of *Das Kapital* was published in Marx's lifetime. Friedrich Engels published two more volumes in 1885 and 1894, after Marx's death.

ers without jobs or money for food.) Taken together, the uprisings were called the Revolution of 1848. No workers gained political power—police and troops restored order everywhere—but to government authorities, the prospect of future violence was frightening, and made writers who advocated revolution, as Marx did, seem extremely dangerous.

Following publication of *The Communist Manifesto,* Marx moved from city to city, country to country. At the time, authorities all over Europe were free to deport foreigners whose political opinions they did not like, or found to be dangerous, and Marx was so targeted. Marx was expelled from Belgium and went to Cologne, Germany. He was expelled from Prussia (at the time, an independent state; Germany had not yet become a unified country) after a year and returned to Paris, but only briefly until he was expelled from France yet again. Finally Marx moved to London, England, where the government was more tolerant of his expression of his views. He lived in England for the rest of his life, spending his days conducting research in the British Library, writing, and participating (often at a distance) in the politics of radical groups in Europe.

Marx never earned much money. For much of his life, he depended on the generosity of his friend Friedrich Engels for financial support (Engels's family made money through ownership of English textile mills). Marx earned money by selling articles to newspapers, in both English and German. In the decade 1852–1862 alone he sold 355 articles to the *New York Daily Tribune,* although this work paid poorly.

Karl Marx and the Industrial Revolution

Marx would undoubtedly be the first to say that his philosophy was a direct result of the Industrial Revolution. He

always believed that ideas stemmed from the way people earned their livings, rather than the other way around.

When Marx was writing, from about 1843 to 1880, the Industrial Revolution was in full swing all across northern Europe. Huge numbers of workers had migrated from farms into cities to find work in newly built factories. Often they could only afford to live in overcrowded apartments. Adults competed with children to work for low wages in dark, often dangerous mills and factories. Wages were barely enough to buy food, and vacations were unheard of. As new machinery was introduced and automation eliminated the need for many workers, employees often lost their jobs on short notice with no hope of bringing in money until they found another job. Sometimes they were evicted from their company-owned housing.

Marx referred to these workers as the *proletariat,* a French word meaning the lowest class of industrial workers who owned no property and had to sell their labor to live. He

Karl Marx believed that laborers should seize factories and run them for the common good, rather than financial gain.
Reproduced by permission of the Library of Congress.

was one of many theorists who addressed these social problems from the workers' viewpoint. His solution was for the workers to revolt, to seize the factories and run them for the common good of society.

Marx thought that his predictions were inevitable. It was a law of history, he wrote, that capitalism (the private ownership of factories) would give rise to its opposite: communism. Driving this change was class warfare, the struggle between groups of people for economic domination. Marx and Engels wrote in their famous political statement *The Communist Manifesto*:

> The history of all hitherto existing society is the history of class struggles.
>
> Freeman and slave, patrician [aristocrat] and plebian [ordinary citizen], lord and serf, guild-master and journeyman, in a word, oppressor and oppressed, stood in constant opposition to one another, carried on an uninterrupted, now hidden, now open fight, a fight that each time ended, either in a revolutionary re-constitution of society at large, or in the common ruin of the contending classes.

Some of Marx's ideas generated especially strong and emotional opposition. His famous statement that "religion is the opiate of the people" enraged the religious faithful, who objected to Marx's suggestion that religion was like a mind-numbing drug that helped people tolerate suffering and helped discourage taking action, such as revolting against the social system. Many people, especially Americans, strongly objected to the idea of class warfare between working people and wealthy property owners. After all, Americans had the assertion in the Declaration of Independence that "all men are created equal" and the right to vote to prove it.

The International Workingmen's Association

In 1864 Marx helped organize the International Workingmen's Association, which was widely known as the First International. It was meant to be a political party representing the interests of workers in all countries. In fact, the association was a somewhat raggedy collection of European radicals with a variety of complaints and beliefs. Marx dominated the group from the start, and used the association to push his belief that the interests of workers were the same regardless of their nation. He urged workers to band together across national boundaries to bring about a new world order in which workers would be in control and a single international government structure would be run by, and for the benefit of, working people. Ownership of land and factories would be transferred to this new government. Of course, this idea was not popular with owners of factories and land, or with governments that Marx thought would soon fade away.

Another radical social theorist, a Russian named Mikhail Bakunin (1814–1876), started to compete for leadership of the group. Bakunin advocated an idea called anarchism: instead of a government of the workers, he believed in no government at all, just voluntary associations. Marx and Bakunin were intense rivals for dominance of radicalism in Europe, and in 1872 Marx dissolved the organization rather than let Bakunin and his fellow anarchists seize control of it.

The dissolution of the First International marked the end of Marx's active involvement in politics. Afterwards he limited his activities to corresponding with radicals in Europe and the United States. In the eight years of its existence, the First International had little to show for its efforts.

On the other hand, national political parties advocating a more moderate form of democratic control of the economy did make strides, and they gradually increased their representation in various national parliaments. Over time, these parties managed to pass laws to limit the power of corporate owners and to improve the living conditions of workers. It was a political battle that continues into the twenty-first century.

Getting personal with Karl Marx

Although he was widely influential in the politics of the working class, in many respects Marx led a solitary life, working day after day alone in the British Library, developing his theories of history and politics, and earning a small income from writing newspaper articles.

Marx did not have the sort of personality that made him personally popular. He had a mocking, disdainful sense of humor and was often blunt in his opinions. Some people found him arrogant and disagreeable, often impatient and easily provoked to angry outbursts. He was without doubt well educated. In high school, he studied Greek and Latin. Later, besides his native German, Marx could converse in French and English, and he could read the Spanish, Italian, Dutch, Russian, and Scandinavian languages.

Marx married the daughter of an aristocrat, Jenny von Westphalen, on June 19, 1843. They had a long and, by all accounts, happy marriage, including three daughters whom Marx adored. (Four other children of the Marx's died in infancy or childhood.) Jenny Marx died of cancer at age sixty-seven on December 2, 1881. Toward the end of his own life, Marx had numerous health problems, including with his liver. He suffered from outbreaks of painful sores that made it difficult for him to sit for long periods. Persistent headaches, coughs, toothaches, and eye inflammations also plagued him.

Barred from returning to Prussia during his lifetime, in ill health, lonely, and poor, Marx died in London on March 14, 1883.

For More Information

Books

Eagleton, Terry. *Marx.* New York: Routledge, 1999.

Hook, Sidney. *Reason, Social Myths, and Democracy.* Buffalo, NY: Prometheus Books, 1991.

Marx, Karl. *Economic and Philosophic Manuscripts of 1844.* Translated by Martin Milligan. New York: International Publishers. 1964.

Singer, Peter. *Marx: A Very Short Introduction.* Oxford, U.K., and New York: Oxford University Press, 2000.

Wheen, Francis. *Karl Marx: A Life.* New York: Norton, 2000.

Periodicals

Arendt, Hannah. "Karl Marx and the Tradition of Western Political Thought." *Social Research,* Summer 2002, p. 273.

Hamilton, Richard F. "*The Communist Manifesto* at 150." *Society,* January 2001, p. 75.

"Karl Marx: The Prophet of Capitalism." *Economist,* December 25, 1999, p. 38.

Marcus, Steven. "Marx's Masterpiece at 150." *New York Times Book Review,* April 26, 1998, p. 39.

Rose, Jonathan. "The Stern, Fiery Father of Communism." *Scholastic Update,* September 22, 1986, p. 13.

Web Sites

"Karl Marx, 1818–1883." *The History Guide: Lectures on Modern European Intellectual History.* http://www.historyguide.org/intellect/marx.html (accessed on February 11, 2003).

"Manifesto of the Communist Party." *Marx/Engels Library.* http://csf.colorado.edu/psn/marx/Archive/1848-CM/ (accessed on February 11, 2003).

"Marx and Engels Internet Archive." *Marxists Internet Archive.* http://www.marxists.org/archive/marx/ (accessed on February 11, 2003).

Cyrus McCormick

Born February 15, 1809
Rockbridge County, Virginia

Died May 13, 1884
Chicago, Illinois

American inventor

"The reaping machine from the United States is the most valuable contribution from abroad, to the stock of our previous knowledge, that we have yet discovered."

—London Times, *1851, commenting on Cyrus McCormick's major invention, the mechanical reaper.*

Reproduced by permission of the Library of Congress.

American inventor and businessman Cyrus McCormick is widely credited with inventing the mechanical reaper, a machine for harvesting grain crops, which greatly expanded the amount of work one farmer could accomplish, revolutionizing U.S. agriculture.

Anyone who eats a bowl of cereal for breakfast or a sandwich for lunch has been affected by McCormick. It was McCormick who took a design developed by his father, Robert McCormick, for an automated reaper, improved it, and sold it to farmers across the United States. In a larger sense, McCormick brought the benefits of the Industrial Revolution, a period marked by the widespread replacement of manual labor by machines that began in Great Britain in the middle of the eighteenth century, to agriculture. The wheat used to make cereal and bread, among other things, was produced at a low cost thanks to the machinery initially developed by McCormick.

An inventive father

Cyrus McCormick was the son of Robert McCormick, who, like Cyrus, had been born on the family estate, called

The Vocabulary of Farming

In the United States at the turn of the twenty-first century, only 2 percent of the population lived and worked on a farm. The vocabulary of farming had become unfamiliar with many people who had never been anywhere near a farm.

The first step in raising crops is to plow the land. This means digging into the earth so that seeds can be planted beneath the surface of the soil. Rather than dig individual holes for each seed, farmers carve long, parallel strips into the soil. One such strip is called a furrow. The machine used for this purpose is also called a plow. Plows were once pulled across the field by horses or oxen; today, they are pulled by huge machines called tractors.

The crops grow until they are ripe. Next comes the harvest, the process of cutting the plants or picking the fruit and vegetables so that they can be brought to market and used for foods. This process differs depending on the crop. Fruits are picked from trees or bushes (usually by hand), and often workers travel from state to state to do this work. (They are called migrant workers.)

Other crops, like wheat (the raw material for flour, which is the essential ingredient of bread), grow like very tall grass. The cutting down of wheat is called reaping, and it is what Cyrus McCormick's invention was intended to do. Before the invention of the reaper, the wheat was cut by hand, using a tool called a scythe (pronounced SITHE). Since plants start to rot not too long after they are ripe, reaping must be done in a short period of time, which is what made McCormick's invention so useful.

In the case of wheat, the seeds that are ground to make flour must be removed from the stem, a process called threshing.

Walnut Grove. Cyrus's mother was Mary Ann Hall (known as Polly) McCormick. Cyrus was one of eight children, and as a boy he occasionally helped out in the blacksmith's shop maintained on the farm.

The McCormicks were a prosperous family. According to tax records, when Cyrus was three years old, his father owned four slaves and seven horses, as well as a cider mill, a distillery, two mills for grinding grain, a sawmill, and a smokehouse. The family lived in a log cabin with Robert's father, but by 1822 Robert had built a brick manor house on the farm, complete with fine furniture bought in Lynchburg and Richmond, Virginia.

Robert McCormick was an inventor as well as a farmer, and he often worked on small gadgets. In the early nineteenth century, as the Industrial Revolution was just gaining momentum in the United States, isolated farmers often had to manufacture their own farm implements and tools since there was no readily available source of mass-produced goods.

One of the projects Robert worked on was a reaper, a machine used to harvest wheat. Wheat, which looks like tall strands of grass when it is growing, had been cut by hand with a sickle, which looks like a large curved knife, or a scythe. Using these tools, one worker could cut between one-half and one acre of wheat in a full day of hard work. Robert wanted to invent a machine that could do this work more efficiently.

By 1809, the year Cyrus was born, Robert was already working on his project, as he would do for the next twenty years. In 1830 Robert applied for a patent (guaranteeing an inventor the exclusive right to earn money from an invention) on a machine he called a "hemp-break," which was a device for dealing with hemp and flax plants. He had also developed machines for threshing (the process of knocking loose the seeds of a wheat plant, which are then ground into flour for making bread); a new sort of bellows, used by blacksmiths to blow air into their fires; and a plow that could be used on hillsides.

The McCormick reaper appears

By all accounts, 1831 was a critical year in the life of Cyrus McCormick and the development of the reaper. In a story later told by Cyrus himself, he worked frantically, day and night, for six weeks to develop a model of a mechanical reaper in the summer of 1831. By the account of other family members, Cyrus was given the plans for a working reaper developed by his father, Robert, over the previous twenty years. The plans were given on one condition: that Cyrus share the benefits of the invention with other members of the family.

In 1834, after making improvements on his father's invention (or improvements on his own invention, in Cyrus's version of the story), Cyrus took out a patent on the first mechanical reaper.

The mechanical reaper sold by Cyrus McCormick helped revolutionize farming in the United States and across the world, enabling farmers to harvest more land at a quicker pace. *Reproduced by permission of the Bettmann Archive/Newsphotos, Inc.*

At first, McCormick made reapers himself in the blacksmith shop on the family farm. But the demand was so strong, the shop could not keep up with the orders. In the meantime, during the 1840s there was an enormous flow of settlers spreading onto the fields of the Midwest, which proved to be among the most fertile farmland in the world. Sensing opportunity, McCormick moved to Chicago, Illinois, which was closer to the rapidly growing market. There, in 1847, he opened a factory to produce reapers in far greater numbers than was possible on his family's Virginia farm.

However, McCormick's success depended on more than a clever invention. He was an aggressive businessman and tireless promoter. In 1851 the McCormick reaper won the Gold Medal at the Crystal Palace Exhibition in London, England, and McCormick became known around the world.

Growing demand

McCormick's reaper found a ready market in the Midwest. Soon after moving to Chicago from Virginia, he sent for his brothers, Leander and William, to join him in Chicago. Initially McCormick's brothers were salaried workers, but in 1859 they demanded a share of the business—it was, after all, based on the invention of their father, they claimed—and McCormick

John Deere's Plow

Cyrus McCormick was not the only inventor who had an impact on agriculture during the Industrial Revolution. John Deere (1804–1886) was a contemporary of McCormick who also contributed to the productivity of farmers.

Deere, born in Rutland, Vermont, became a blacksmith's apprentice (student helper) in nearby Middlebury, Vermont, at age seventeen. In the nineteenth century, blacksmiths performed a wide variety of tasks for America's mostly rural population. Most notably they made horseshoes. But blacksmiths also made pots and pans for farmers and many other household and farm implements made of metal.

In 1836, facing financial ruin as a result of fires that burned down two of his blacksmithing shops, Deere moved west, to Grand Detour, Illinois, where he set up a new blacksmithing business.

Deere discovered that plows designed for use in the East were ill-suited to the heavier soils of the Midwest. He developed a new plow that used steel (originally from an old circular saw) instead of wood for the "moldboard," the part of a plow that lifts and turns the soil after it has been cut by the blade. Whereas the soil of the Midwest would stick to the old wooden moldboards, it fell away from Deere's new metal moldboard.

Deere's design was an immediate success. From his first design, in 1837, Deere and a partner were producing one thousand such plows a year by 1847. It was in 1847 that Deere sold his interest in the business to his partner and opened a new company in Moline, Illinois. He introduced a further improvement by ordering special hard steel from England. Within a decade, his company was selling ten thousand of the improved plows a year.

In 1868 Deere organized his business into Deere and Company. The company today sells products in 160 countries and dates its beginnings to Deere's original blacksmith shop opened in 1837.

gave each brother 25 percent of the business. In 1859 the business was named Cyrus H. McCormick and Brothers.

The business boomed as the population of farmers in the Midwest grew rapidly. One driving factor was the nature of the work performed by the reaper: it harvested crops. In farming, when crops are ready for harvesting, they need to be brought in quickly so that they do not rot in the field. As the size of farms expanded on the flat fields of the Midwest, bringing in large harvests quickly called for an effective machine, and McCormick's harvester answered this need.

During the next two decades, McCormick's business grew rapidly despite minor setbacks. In 1871, for example, McCormick's factory and home burned to the ground in the great Chicago fire. In 1879 another reorganization resulted in the formation of the McCormick Harvesting Machine Company, a company that eventually was named International Harvester (and is today called Navistar International Corporation). Cyrus McCormick remained head of the company, and shortly after this reorganization his brother Leander retired from active participation in the business.

The impact of Cyrus McCormick

As his company grew and prospered, McCormick introduced a series of new and improved machines. The successive models of his reaper added tasks (such as threshing and binding the grain), further reducing manpower. At first, all of his machines were pulled by horses or oxen; later models were designed to be pulled by a mechanical tractor.

Farmers equipped with McCormick's machines—and equipment made by other innovators, like John Deere (see box on page 92)—prospered because they could farm more land with less labor than farmers not so equipped. Mechanized farming is the main reason for the steep decline of the proportion of Americans engaged in farming for a living.

McCormick pioneered more than just the use of machines on farms. He was among the first to give loans to farmers, making it easier for them to pay for expensive machines. He also advertised extensively to promote his machines and himself. These business techniques contributed perhaps as much to McCormick's success as to the success of the mechanical devices he developed. They also helped change the face of the North American continent and made the American Midwest the "breadbasket of the world."

For More Information

Books

Kozar, Richard. *Inventors and Their Discoveries.* Philadelphia, PA: Chelsea House Publishers, 1999.

McCormick, Cyrus Hall. *The Century of the Reaper.* Boston, MA: Houghton Mifflin Company, 1931.

Periodicals

Duffy, Bruce. "Harvest of Stubbornness." *D & B Reports,* May–June, 1993, p. 58.

Weisberger, Bernard. "The Forgotten Four Hundred: Chicago's First Millionaires." *American Heritage,* November 1987, p. 34.

Web Sites

"Cyrus McCormick: Agricultural Inventor." *Teachervision.com.* http://www.teachervision.com/lesson-plans/lesson-4806.html (accessed on February 11, 2003).

"Shenandoah Valley's McCormick Farm." *Shenandoah Valley Agricultural Research and Extension Center.* http://www.vaes.vt.edu/steeles/mccormick/mccormick.html (accessed on February 11, 2003).

J. P. Morgan

Born April 17, 1837
Hartford, Connecticut

Died March 31, 1913
Rome, Italy

American financier

"If you have to ask how much it costs, you can't afford it."

Reproduced by permission of the Library of Congress.

J. P. Morgan built the largest private bank in the United States, and he used his enormous financial clout to assemble some of the largest corporations in the world. He demonstrated, perhaps more than any single individual, the power of finance in the economy of the Industrial Revolution, a period of fast-paced economic change that began in Great Britain in the middle of the eighteenth century.

It is widely believed in the United States that the president is the most powerful man in the country, elected by the people in the world's most powerful democracy. But in the last decade of the nineteenth century and the first decade of the twentieth century, Morgan, a banker, arguably held more power over the nation than the president held over Morgan.

So great was Morgan's financial influence that the government depended on his backing to save it from financial ruin. Even the most powerful and wealthy industrialists of the time, such as **John D. Rockefeller** (1839–1937) and **Andrew Carnegie** (1835–1919; see entries), could not resist Morgan's economic power.

Childhood and early years

Many of the heroes of the industrial age, like Andrew Carnegie and **Henry Ford** (1863–1947; see entry), were self-made men, rising from modest beginnings to leadership of huge industrial enterprises. Morgan was not one of them.

John Pierpont was born on April 17, 1837, in Hartford, Connecticut. While his contemporaries were puttering around in farm workshops or in city slums, Pierpont, as he was called, was living in the lap of luxury.

His father, Junius Spencer Morgan (1813–1890), had been born into a wealthy New England family. Junius had been a merchant when he was hired by an American banker in England, George Peabody. Together the two men created a thriving international bank that directed British investments into the rapidly growing American economy. Junius was intent on instructing his son in the ways of banking and finance so that he could take over the family's fortunes.

To accomplish this, Pierpont was sent to English High School in Boston, Massachusetts, then to the prestigious University of Göttingen in Germany. By the time he was fifteen, Pierpont had already begun collecting art, which became a lifelong obsession. Five years later, in 1857, when Pierpont came home to start his career in banking, he was well educated and sophisticated, having a taste for fine art and high living.

Pierpont's first job was as an accountant at the firm of Duncan, Sherman and Company, which had close ties to London's George Peabody and Company, the firm of Pierpont's father.

A few years later, with the outbreak of the U.S. Civil War (1861–65), Pierpont joined his father's financial ventures. Their goal was to arrange financing for both the U.S. government and for America's rapidly expanding industrial base. Entrepreneurs needed funding to start new companies or expand existing operations in businesses like railroads and steel manufacturing. J. P. Morgan was involved in all of these industries, which defined the new economy of industrialization.

The Morgans were especially active in financing the construction of railroads. Later, when there were too many railroads for the available business, resulting in cutthroat competition, Morgan bought them up and consolidated (combined) them, a practice criticized as creating a monopoly (gaining exclusive ownership or control of an industry), but one that proved necessary for the railroad business to survive.

Morgan worked for Dabney, Morgan and Company from 1864 until 1871, when he joined Drexel, Morgan and Company, which became J. P. Morgan and Company in 1895, by which time it was internationally recognized as one of the most powerful financial institutions in the world.

Morgan the man

By the end of his life, Morgan was famous worldwide for his financial clout (power and influence). Behind his reputation was an outsized personality easily big enough to fill the role he played in the economy of the United States.

Virtually all accounts of Morgan describe him as a large man who dominated every room he entered. He had a booming voice and a large, imposing figure. He was noted for having an exceptionally large nose that, due to a childhood skin disease, was discolored (red or purple, depending on the description). And he was said to have a stare that could intimidate almost anyone.

According to historians, Morgan's successful effort in 1907 to stave off a panic (uncontrolled selling of stocks) on Wall Street consisted of assembling a group of fifty bankers in the library of his home one evening and locking the door. He was intent on raising $25 million to save companies facing financial disaster in the stock panic. Approaching one reluctant banker with a paper committing him to raise money, Morgan ordered him to sign. "There's the place," Morgan boomed, pointing at the paper, "and here's the pen." The banker signed—as did the others in the room. Morgan unlocked the doors at 4:45 in the morning. The panic of 1907 was under control.

Yet for all his ability to dominate, Morgan was refined in his private life. He loved fine clothes, fine art, and elegant surroundings. At age twenty-four, he married a young woman who was suffering from tuberculosis (an infectious lung disease). She died on their honeymoon in Europe.

J.P. Morgan turned Wall Street in New York City (pictured) into the center of the American economy. His role as the nation's most influential banker underlined the importance of finance in creating and maintaining industrial enterprises.
Reproduced by permission of AP/Wide World Photos.

Later, he married again, but the marriage to Frances Louise was not a happy one. Although they had several children, Morgan and his wife usually arranged to be on different continents. And while his father had taken special care to instruct his son in the ways of the banking business, Morgan took just the opposite approach with his own son, regularly ignoring him in favor of other men in making business appointments. (Morgan's son succeeded him and became an important figure on Wall Street, but he lived in his father's shadow and lacked his father's dominating personality.)

Morgan the mogul

More than any other single person, Morgan brought about a dramatic shift in the American economy and introduced a profound change in the Industrial Revolution: he made finance king of the economy.

Before Morgan's time, the largest American business enterprises had been built from scratch by entrepreneurs, many of them engineers, who built things. Andrew Carnegie knew about building steel, and relentlessly pursued better ways of doing it. **Cyrus McCormick** (1809–1884; see entry) knew about designing and making mechanical reapers.

Morgan knew about money, and the power that money could wield over business. When Morgan started out, most large industrial enterprises had their headquarters in the towns or cities where the business had been started, often in a garage or shed where their inventor-founders had fiddled with tools and machines. By the time Morgan died, in 1913, most big American corporations had their headquarters in New York, in order to be close to the source of finance, which was on Wall Street. (Morgan's banking headquarters was located on Wall Street, right next to the New York Stock Exchange.)

Although he was widely criticized by some as a robber baron (a wealthy industrialist or businessman who used unscrupulous business practices) during his lifetime, Morgan played a crucial role in the creation of the industrial giants that dominated the world economy during the twentieth century. It was the House of Morgan that arranged to finance the creation of companies like American Telephone and Telegraph (AT&T), International Harvester (successor to Cyrus McCormick's company), General Electric, Westinghouse, and, most famously, United States Steel (see box on page 101).

Morgan played a central role in the transformation of the American economy from a collection of huge firms

J.P. Morgan (left) talks with lawyer Thomas Lamont and Senator John Davis before a 1933 Senate Banking Committee hearing. *Reproduced by permission of AP/Wide World Photos.*

owned by wealthy individuals, typically their founders, to an economy of large corporations owned by stockholders. Morgan's role was to use his bank's funds to assemble the corporation, then to sell shares to the public.

From an economical viewpoint, these giant industrial enterprises were well equipped to compete globally and propelled the U.S. economy to become the largest in the world. Over several decades, this development also transformed corporations from companies that operated entirely outside the oversight, or control, of any but their wealthy owners to institutions that published every detail of their operations for the benefit of millions of stockholders, large and small. In the twenty-first century, significant shares of corporations are still owned by large retirement funds that invest for the benefit of millions of individual workers.

Thus, American business became far more democratic and subject to public scrutiny than ever before. This was not an aim of Morgan's, but it was an unintended result.

United States Steel: The First Billion-Dollar Company

In 1901 J. P. Morgan paid Andrew Carnegie $480 million to acquire Carnegie Steel Company, a leading steel maker. Carnegie's steel company was the centerpiece of a company Morgan named United States Steel, which was the result of Morgan's consolidation of several smaller firms into a single giant corporation that dominated the industry.

Shortly after buying Carnegie's company, which had stood in the way of Morgan achieving a virtual monopoly on steel production, Morgan sold shares in the new company (for which he paid about $800 million in total) for $1.3 billion. U.S. Steel thus became the first billion-dollar corporation in the United States.

The story of how Morgan bought Carnegie's company demonstrated how business was done in the era.

Morgan, who thought that competition was inefficient and therefore bad (because it tended to lower prices), met Charles Schwab, the president of Carnegie Steel, in the library of his home on Madison Avenue. Morgan asked Schwab to find out how much Carnegie wanted for his steel company.

The next day, while Carnegie was playing golf, Schwab asked the question. Carnegie thought about it overnight, then wrote a number on a piece of paper—$480 million—and gave the paper to Schwab, who took it to Morgan.

The banker glanced at the paper and instantly announced: "I accept this price." Less than three months later, the deal was signed and Morgan created U.S. Steel.

Some time later, encountering Morgan on a transatlantic voyage, Carnegie told the banker that he thought he could have gotten $100 million more if he had asked for it. "Very likely," Morgan replied.

Morgan the public servant

On at least two occasions, Morgan intervened in the financial markets to avert disaster. In 1895 American populists, mostly farmers seeking economic reforms, conducted a campaign against the gold standard, the policy whereby every dollar issued by the U.S. Treasury had to be backed by a certain amount of gold. In theory, anyone could hand over a dollar bill and obtain a certain amount of gold from the government. The policy had the effect of limiting the amount of money in circulation, and therefore making it more difficult and expensive to obtain loans, which farmers needed to pay for planting their crops.

The campaign against the gold standard, led by William Jennings Bryan (1860–1925) of Nebraska, caused a "run" on the treasury in 1895. (Investors became afraid their dollars would no longer be convertible to gold bullion, or bulk gold, and tried to cash in while they still could.) The run raised the possibility that the U.S. government would not be able to pay its debts. Morgan intervened by raising a $62 million loan for the government, which eased the fears of investors and maintained the credit-rating standing of the government.

Twelve years later, a panic on Wall Street caused investors to sell their stocks even as stock prices plunged, threatening an economic catastrophe. Again, Morgan stepped in and raised $25 million to be used to rescue companies threatened with financial collapse. (This was the aforementioned occasion on which Morgan locked investors in his private library until they agreed to contribute to the fund.)

In the twenty-first century, the Federal Reserve Bank fills the role that Morgan played. Morgan had enough money to be able, and willing, to avert bank failures or financial panic by lending money or supplying cash in an emergency, much as the government began doing with establishment of the Federal Reserve Bank in 1913. In this way, Morgan had greater financial power than either the U.S. president or the Congress.

Morgan the art collector

Many of the robber barons of the Industrial Revolution were harshly condemned for accumulating vast fortunes even as their workers lived in severe poverty. But most also engaged in philanthropy by donating money to worthy causes. Morgan was no exception.

While Andrew Carnegie is famous for donating most of his fortune to establish more than two thousand public libraries, among other institutions, Morgan was a world-famous collector of art.

Beginning as a teenager, Morgan was an avid collector. He bought Gutenberg Bibles, famous European paintings, medieval tapestries, and Chinese porcelains. It was estimated that he had spent $60 million on art by the time of his death, equivalent to $1 billion in 2002 dollars.

J.P. Morgan spent millions of dollars collecting European paintings, sculptures, and other works of art. Upon his death, much of his collection was given to the Metropolitan Museum of Art in New York City (pictured). *Reproduced by permission of the Corbis Corporation.*

Upon his death, Morgan contributed much of his collection to the Metropolitan Museum of Art in New York (he had served as president of the museum during his lifetime). Other Morgan collections can be seen at the Morgan Library in New York City.

The heritage of Morgan

If Morgan had not existed, he would have had to have been invented. While many of the megacorporations he created, as a means of minimizing competition and chaos in the economic marketplace, have faded or disappeared, the concept of finance as the key feature of economies has not. Nor has the legacy of those companies that put the U.S. economy at the top of the world during most of the twentieth century.

Morgan was famously opposed to competition, but his reason was not simply to increase profits and his own wealth. He greatly disliked disorder and unpredictability in the marketplace and felt that business competition created chaos. He hated the way Andrew Carnegie constantly drove down the price of steel, thereby jeopardizing his competitors—and their employees. Better by far, Morgan thought, to control industries in a trust (a group of corporations with monopoly control) in order to avoid disorder.

Morgan himself, it turned out, was not nearly as wealthy as some of his contemporaries. He paid Andrew Carnegie $480 million for his steel business, and at the time of his death John D. Rockefeller was said to be worth about $1 billion ($190 billion in 2002 values). Morgan died with an estate of about $80 million; hardly a pauper but not in the league of a Rockefeller or Carnegie. Legend has it that when he heard about Morgan's estate, Rockefeller sniffed: "And to think, he wasn't even a rich man."

But while he was alive, Morgan was the national symbol of wealth. He was often denounced by Congressmen, and resented by ordinary citizens. In New York, the nation's financial capital, he was known as Jupiter, after the most powerful god of Roman mythology.

Since Morgan, no single individual has played the same role in American business. Morgan was unique in bringing a larger-than-life personality to bear on the economy, and thus on the lives of millions of Americans.

For More Information

Books

Carosso, Vincent P. *The Morgans: Private International Bankers, 1854–1913.* Cambridge, MA: Harvard University Press, 1987.

Diaz Espino, Ovidio. *How Wall Street Created a Nation: J. P. Morgan, Teddy Roosevelt, and the Panama Canal.* New York: Four Walls Eight Windows, 2001.

Strouse, Jean. *Morgan: American Financier.* New York: HarperPerennial, 2000.

Periodicals

Chernow, Ron. "Blessed Barons." *Time,* December 7, 1998, p. 74.

"The Making of the Modern Company." *Business Week,* August 28, 2000, p. 98.

Samuelson, Robert J. "J. P. Morgan Rises Again: What America's Most Powerful of Private Bankers Taught Us Is That, in Business, Finance and in Life, It's Character That Really Counts." *Newsweek,* August 12, 2002, p. 43.

Web Sites

"The Gilded Age." *A Classification of American Wealth: History and Genealogy of the Wealthy Families of America.* http://www.raken.com/american_wealth/Gilded_age_index5.asp (accessed on February 11, 2003).

Rousmaniere, John. "Commodore J. Pierpont Morgan." *New York Yacht Club.* http://www.nyyc.org/Images/Heritage%20Series/Morgan.htm (accessed on February 11, 2003).

Samuel F. B. Morse

Born April 27, 1791
Charlestown, Massachusetts

Died April 2, 1872
New York, New York

American inventor

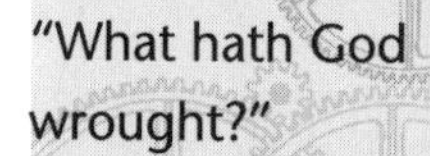

"What hath God wrought?"

—First long-distance telegraph message, transmitted from Washington, D.C., to Baltimore, Maryland.

Reproduced by permission of the Library of Congress

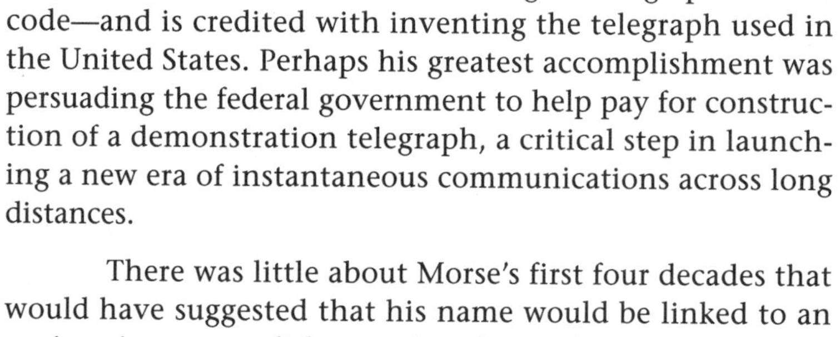

Samuel Finley Breese Morse gave his name to a long-dominant means of communicating via telegraph—Morse code—and is credited with inventing the telegraph used in the United States. Perhaps his greatest accomplishment was persuading the federal government to help pay for construction of a demonstration telegraph, a critical step in launching a new era of instantaneous communications across long distances.

There was little about Morse's first four decades that would have suggested that his name would be linked to an engineering accomplishment that changed the way the world communicated—and even foretold the era of E-mail over the Internet. Nevertheless, it is Morse who is credited with inventing Morse code, a method of communication that uses a series of dots and dashes—short sounds and longer ones—that is fundamentally similar to the zeros and ones used by today's computers communicating over the Internet.

Rapid long-distance communications may not seem, at first, like a central part of the Industrial Revolution, a period of fast-paced economic development that began in Great Britain in the middle of the eighteenth century. But as soon as production of finished goods started to become centralized in factories, new needs arose in communications. Factories needed to order supplies from far away, as well as receive orders from distant customers. Business owners saw an advantage in quickly finding out about price changes in manufactured goods or raw materials, or about other developments affecting the supply and demand of goods. And fast-moving trains needed a way to control traffic and avoid head-on collisions when there was only one set of rails shared by trains going in both directions.

At the time when Morse developed his famous code, he was one of many people working on the concept. It was, in the end, not just his code, or the invention of the telegraph itself that counted. What counted was Morse's success in selling the idea to the U.S. Congress, persuading the government to help him fund the project, and thereby attracting world attention to his first message sent over a primitive telegraph system from Washington, D.C., to Baltimore, Maryland.

Early life as a painter

Samuel Morse, known to his family by his middle name, Finley, was born in Charlestown, Massachusetts, outside Boston, in 1791. His father was a Congregationalist minister who was highly regarded but not highly paid. Morse attended Yale University, from which he graduated in 1810. While there, he learned something of the then-new science of electricity, and he made some primitive batteries.

But science was not his chief interest; he was fascinated by art. Morse returned to the Boston area after graduation and took a job as a clerk in a bookstore. Shortly afterward he traveled to London, England, to study art. In the four years he spent in London, Morse got off to a good start. He won a prestigious award—the gold medal in a competition sponsored by the Adelphi Society of Art—and he studied under two American masters, Benjamin West (1738–1820) and Washington Allston (1779–1843), who were living in London at the time.

In 1815, though, his parents could no longer afford to help pay for his life abroad, and Morse reluctantly returned home. His plan was to earn a living by painting grand depictions of historical events, but he discovered there was not much money to be made in this area. Instead, in the era before photography, people who could afford it commissioned Morse to paint small portraits of themselves. Morse succeeded at this, painting such prominent figures as President James Monroe (1758–1831), the poet William Cullen Bryant (1794–1878), and **Eli Whitney** (1765–1825; see entry), inventor of the cotton gin. But he did not earn a lot of money at this sort of painting, and in any case he considered it an inferior form of art. He had an idea to paint a large scene featuring the entire U.S. House of Representatives, with recognizable portraits of about eighty members, but he could not find financial support.

Despite failure to achieve financial success as a painter, Morse was one of thirty artists who founded the National Academy of Design in New York City in 1826. Morse was elected president of the academy, and held the office for thirty-nine years, long after his interests had turned to another subject: the telegraph.

Passing time on an ocean cruise

Morse returned to Europe for three years, from 1829 to 1832, to perfect his painting technique. On his return, he settled in New York City, where he was appointed professor of the arts at the University of the City of New York (now called New York University).

It was in 1832, sailing home from his second European visit, that Morse heard of a new discovery: the electromagnet. The English scientist Michael Faraday (1791-1867) had discovered that electric current passing through a coil of wire could magnetize a piece of metal and cause it to attract metal objects. This gave Morse an idea: by varying electric current flowing through a wire, a magnet many miles away could move a piece of metal. And that metal could record a message, for example, by tapping a strip of paper.

The telegraph, as it was eventually developed, thus combined two ideas: electromagnetism and its ability to move objects remotely; and a scheme to translate those movements into words.

Morse's idea was to use a combination of short and long electric pulses to transmit a message. Each letter of the alphabet would be represented as a unique combination of long and short impulses—dots and dashes as they were later called. These combinations made up Morse code.

For example, the letter "e" is represented by a single dot: • . An "a" is a dot and a dash: • - . An "s" is three dots: • • • . A "y" is represented by a dash followed by a dot followed by two dashes: - • - -. The word "easy" would therefore be sent as the sequence • / • - / • • • / - • - - .

It took Morse—about three years, until 1835, to get his first model telegraph working. He used materials he found at hand: an old canvas stretcher, a home-made battery, the works from an old clock.

Morse was not the first person to get a telegraph-like device working. Models had been proposed and implemented as early as 1753. But most of the earlier models involved multiple wires; the first one required twenty-six wires, one for each letter of the alphabet. In 1833 German engineers developed a model that required only five wires. Morse's innovation was to reduce the number of wires to one; he did this through the famous code that bears his name.

Money, please

Morse's second great contribution to the advancement of rapid communications was his 1842 success in persuading the U.S. Congress to contribute federal government funds to help build a single-wire telegraph

Samuel Morse the Politician

The success of the telegraph brought Samuel Morse fame and wealth, and soon, his interests turned to politics. Morse had a brief and unsuccessful political career in New York, running for office as a Nativist, one who favors native inhabitants as opposed to immigrants. He ran for mayor of New York City in 1836, garnering 1,550 votes, and again in 1841, when he received fewer than 100 votes.

The Nativists, who were also known as "Know-Nothings," were disturbed by the surge of immigrants into the United States in the middle third of the nineteenth century. Many of the immigrants were from countries other than England, and they began to change the face of the American population.

The platform of the Nativists included intense nationalism (sometimes called jingoism), racism, opposition to immigration, and opposition to Catholics and Jews. Morse made no apologies for views that in the early twenty-first century would be unacceptable to the majority of Americans.

In particular, he was fiercely anti-Catholic and, because many Irish immigrants were Catholics, anti-Irish. Morse favored denying citizenship to people born outside of the United States. He also wrote pamphlets opposing those who would abolish slavery.

line between Washington, D.C., and Baltimore, Maryland. Congress agreed to pay $30,000 (the equivalent of about $500,000 in 2000) to string the wire.

On May 11, 1844, Morse used the wire to send what is regarded as the first telegraph message from city to city. Sitting in the U.S. Supreme Court, Morse sent his famous first message a distance of forty-one miles to the Mount Clair train station in Baltimore. The text was a passage from a Bible owned by the daughter of the commissioner of patents: "What hath God wrought?"

Further demonstrations soon followed. People sent their names by telegraph from Baltimore to Washington and saw them come back again within a minute. Two people forty miles apart conducted an argument via telegraph messages. Results of a Democratic convention in Baltimore reached the nation's capital almost immediately. To people in the 1840s, the telegraph was nothing less than a miracle of instant communications.

Although the first telegraph message is closely linked to Morse, he was not the only person involved in its success. Morse was not an engineer by training, and he received advice and help from others, notably his assistants Alfred Vail and William Baxter, and the American physicist Joseph Henry (1797–1878), who demonstrated a working telegraph in 1831, a full year before Morse even got started. Europeans also had made advances in telegraphy, especially Louis Breguet (1804–1883) of France. It was Vail who received Morse's famous first message in Baltimore, and he is often credited with refining Morse's code to the famous pattern of dots and dashes, which enabled a receiver to "hear" a message and transcribe it into letters. (Morse's original machine printed the dots and dashes on a long, thin strip of paper, from which the code was then interpreted by sight.)

Nevertheless, it was Morse who filed for a patent, which guarantees the inventor exclusive rights to make money on the invention, for a printing telegraph in 1844; the patent was granted in 1849.

The impact of the telegraph

Although it took Morse years to get the funding to string a telegraph wire between Baltimore, Maryland, and

A telegraph operator is depicted translating messages sent by wire. The telegraph enabled quicker means of communication across the expanding United States. *Reproduced by permission of The Library of Congress.*

Washington, D.C., his invention spread across the country fairly quickly after that first message was transmitted. Within ten years there were about twenty-three thousand miles of telegraph wire in operation, mostly following the route of railroad tracks. By 1868 the first underwater cable linking Europe and the United States had been laid.

Like many inventors, Morse complained about having to defend his patents against businesspeople who wanted to exploit the invention without paying for it. Eventually, Morse became a shareholder in the American Telegraph Company, which became the dominant company offering telegraphy in the United States.

Other inventors continued to make improvements, notably by multiplexing, or sending multiple messages across one wire at the same time. One of Thomas Edison's (1847–1931) first inventions was something called a stock ticker, in essence a machine that printed stock prices sent by telegraph.

Rapid communications was a critical component to the development of the Industrial Revolution. Combined with the spread of railroads, it enabled companies to expand greatly the market for their products. Merchants could order manufactured goods from hundreds, or thousands, of miles away, and expect confirmation within hours; delivery came shortly thereafter as the railroads expanded their service. Especially for a geographically large area such as the United States, the telegraph was a key development in the growth of manufacturing.

The telegraph also played a key role in the operation of financial markets, enabling investors across the country virtually "real-time" access to stock prices and news that might affect their decision to invest in one company or another. The ability to tap the savings and investment of the entire country became crucial in raising the huge amounts of capital (money) needed to sustain the Industrial Revolution.

In his later years, Morse was a noted philanthropist, one who benefits others through charitable gifts. The telegraph operators of the United States honored Morse with a bronze statue in New York's Central Park in 1871. Morse died in New York the following year.

For More Information

Books

Coe, Lewis. *The Telegraph: A History of Morse's Invention and Its Predecessors in the United States.* Jefferson, NC: McFarland, 1993.

Hays, Wilma Pitchford. *Samuel Morse and the Electronic Age.* New York: Watts, 1966.

Kerby, Mona. *Samuel Morse.* New York: F. Watts, 1991.

Periodicals

Forbes, Steve. "Telegraphic Lesson: Don't Depend on Uncle Sam." *Forbes,* July 5, 1993, p. 26.

Frost, George. "Let's Remember Sam." *Journal of the Patent and Trademark Office Society,* April 1994, p. 277.

Web Sites

"The Invention Dimension: Samuel F. B. Morse" *Massachusetts Institute of Technology.* http://web.mit.edu/invent/iow/morse.html (accessed on February 13, 2003).

Locust Grove, the Samuel F. B. Morse Historic Site. http://www.morsehistoricsite.org/ (accessed on February 13, 2003).

"The Papers of Samuel F. B. Morse." *American Memory, Library of Congress.* http://memory.loc.gov/ammem/atthtml/mrshome.html (accessed on February 13, 2003).

"I aimed at the public's heart, and by accident I hit it in the stomach."

—Upton Sinclair, on the public reaction to his 1906 novel The Jungle.

The Muckrakers

Jacob Riis

Born May 3, 1849
Ribe, Denmark

Died May 26, 1914
Barre, Massachusetts

Lincoln Steffens

Born April 6, 1866
Sacramento, California

Died August 9, 1936
Carmel, California

Upton Sinclair

Born September 20, 1878
Baltimore, Maryland

Died November 25, 1968
Bound Brook, New Jersey

Ida Tarbell

Born November 5, 1857
Hatch Hallow, Pennsylvania

Died January 6, 1944
Bridgeport, Connecticut

American journalists

Jacob Riis, Upton Sinclair, Lincoln Steffens, and Ida Tarbell were the best-known of the so-called muckrakers, crusading journalists active from about 1890 to 1910 (and in some cases, many years longer) who helped to bring about a number of governmental reforms. Writing for newspapers (Riis) and magazines (Steffens and Tarbell), or publishing novels (Sinclair), these writers specialized in writing stories about the suffering of underpaid workers, government corruption, and shady dealings by business executives like **John D. Rockefeller** (1839–1937; see entry). By bringing these stories to light, the muckrakers encouraged strong corrective action to be taken by government.

Origin of the word "muckraker"

The term muckraker was first used by President **Theodore Roosevelt** (1858–1919; see entry), and it was not one of praise or commendation (although Roosevelt was a friend of Jacob Riis's). It literally means to rake out muck (manure or filth). The muckrakers were writers who wrote about

Nutcrackers

"The railroads are unjust to farmers!"

As a farmer you are sick and tired of being taken advantage of and by the railroads and rich business men who run them.

Write a letter to your local newspaper expressing your thoughts around this one idea. Back up your opinions with facts from the book (p220). What are your economic problems? What are some ways you can fight the railroads?

Magazine articles by journalists known as "muckrakers" exposed the harsh working conditions faced by thousands of children during the Industrial Revolution. *Reproduced by permission of the Library of Congress.*

the desperate living conditions, primarily in cities such as New York and Chicago, experienced by mostly immigrant workers during the late nineteenth and early twentieth centuries. They engaged their readers with tales of crooked politicians bribed by businessmen to look the other way when rotten beef was distributed by meatpacking plants, for example. The muckrakers helped the public understand how the megafortunes of their era had been gained through ruthless dealings and at the expense of thousands of competitors driven out of business and workers employed at very low wages. With the muckrackers' help, a period of uncontrolled and unchecked industrial development came to an end in the United States.

Each of the muckrakers was best-known for a particular target:

- Jacob Riis documented the desperate living conditions of people in New York City's Lower East Side slums.
- Upton Sinclair used fiction as his vehicle to attack social ills. His best-known novel, *The Jungle* (1906), was written to promote the cause of socialism (a political system in which the government controls the major industries) as a cure for the ills of American society. But the story, focusing on the stockyards of Chicago and contaminated beef, proved highly effective in promoting federal regulation of food processing.
- Lincoln Steffens focused on corrupt municipal (local government) officials in several major cities.
- Ida Tarbell's story of John D. Rockefeller's Standard Oil Company was instrumental in building public outrage at the abuses of business owners who tried to suppress competition in an industry.

The muckrakers did not represent a single political viewpoint. Sinclair, for example, believed in socialism, the political philosophy that government should control business. Tarbell, on the other hand, famous for uncovering the abusive practices of Rockefeller, one of the biggest businessmen of the era, felt friendly towards many businessmen, and ended her career writing glowing biographies of business leaders.

But from 1890 to 1910, these writers contributed to a profound shift in American political thinking. The attitude that government had no right to interfere with business changed as these writers brought to light the inhumane conditions of women and children working in factories, or the filthy, unsanitary conditions of meatpacking plants in Chicago. Articles written by the muckrakers revealing such practices caused a public outcry for government regulation and control over business practices.

Jacob Riis and the slums of New York

Jacob Riis. *Reproduced by permission of the Library of Congress.*

Jacob Riis was born in the small town of Ribe, Denmark, in 1849. He became one of millions of Europeans who immigrated to the United States in the latter half of the nineteenth century, hoping to find a bright future and economic opportunity. Riis found a much harsher reality, and documented it with photographs and essays.

Jacob was one of fourteen children born to Niels Edward Riis and Caroline Riis. His father taught in a Latin school, which Jacob attended as a boy, occasionally helping his father prepare stories for a weekly newspaper. According to a legend told about Jacob's youth, at age thirteen he came across the home of a poor family in his hometown. So horrified was young Jacob at conditions in which the family lived, he spent his own money to buy soap and paint to clean up the house, which was infested with rats. As a teenager Riis moved to Copenhagen, the Danish capital, where he became a learning assistant (apprentice) to a carpenter. Looking for a brighter future, he decided to immigrate to America in 1870, arriving in New York when he was twenty-one.

There, the harsh reality of the New World took hold. Riis needed money to live, and so he took any job that came his way. He tried farming, coal mining, brick making, and peddling from a cart. Occasionally he had to spend the night in a noisy and dirty homeless shelter.

After four years of the rough-and-tumble life of an immigrant, Riis found an editing job at a small newspaper, the *South Brooklyn News*. Three years later, in 1877, he was hired as a reporter for the *New York Tribune* and assigned to cover the slums of the Lower East Side of Manhattan, a borough of New York City.

Riis married a childhood sweetheart from Ribe, Elizabeth Nielsen, and they had five children. Elizabeth died in 1905, and two years later he married Mary Phillips, a woman many years younger who had served as his secretary.

The Industrial Revolution, a period of fast-paced economic change that began in Great Britain in the middle of the eighteenth century, was in full swing in the last quarter of the nineteenth century, and in New York thousands of immigrants were employed in small factories, many sewing women's clothing. Workers' wages were barely enough to live, and workers were forced to live in tenements, crowded apartment buildings jammed next to each other block after block.

As a journalist, Riis wrote articles that focused on the everyday lives of New York's poorest workers. He wrote of hunger, lack of sanitation, apartments without heat in winter, dangerous firetraps, and poor treatment of the dead. His stories shed light on living conditions that wealthy New Yorkers could not have imagined.

In 1890 Riis collected some of his newspaper stories and published them in a book, *How the Other Half Lives*. The work resulted in Riis meeting a young Republican politician, Theodore Roosevelt, who had been a federal civil service commissioner and in 1895 became police commissioner of New York City. In that job, Roosevelt quickly developed a reputation as an honest politician who vigorously attacked the corruption and bribery that was commonplace in the slums of New York. Roosevelt and Riis became longtime friends. Roosevelt later offered Riis government positions, but the author preferred to continue his career as writer, photographer, and lecturer.

One of the unique elements of *How the Other Half Lives* is its photography. Riis was among the first journalists to use photos in documenting the living conditions of the poor. For this reason, he is also an important figure in the history of photojournalism.

Riis continued to publish books about slum conditions: *Out of Mulberry Street* (1898), *The Battle with the Slum* (1902), and *Children of the Tenement* (1903). In all these books, he focused on the living conditions of the poor but did not attack the underlying economic system of capitalism (private ownership of goods and property) as the root cause, as did some of his fellow muckrakers.

Riis did not simply write about conditions he chanced upon but actively attempted to relieve the misery he found in the slums. He exposed the fact that water supplies were contaminated, and he campaigned for the city of New York to purchase a large watershed that is used to hold some of the city's water supply today. He worked to abolish the rough and dangerous police-run homeless shelters. By exposing the lives of children working hour upon hour in factories, he pushed for stricter enforcement of child-labor laws.

Riis also fought for laws that set minimum living standards for apartments and the tearing down of dangerous, unhealthful tenements. His work led the city of New York to pass laws requiring minimum standards for dwellings.

In all these efforts, Riis revealed that the economy of the Industrial Revolution had resulted in horrific living conditions for thousands of citizens. He felt that there was no organization besides government to address these ills, and it was among Riis's accomplishments that public attitudes toward government action changed drastically. As citizens became more sympathetic to the plight of the poor, it became easier for politicians to take effective action to help them, such as mandating a minimum wage or maximum hours per day a person could be required to work.

Riis's career was cut short by illness. In 1904, he was stricken with heart disease and forced to restrict his writing and lecturing activities. On May 26, 1914, Riis died at his country home in Barre, Massachusetts.

Upton Sinclair and *The Jungle*

Upton Sinclair was born in Baltimore, Maryland, in 1878, the son of a distinguished Southern family that had fallen onto hard times. His father was an alcoholic who sold liquor for a living. His mother was the daughter of a prominent Baltimore family. The result was a childhood marked by contradiction—upper-middle-class culture on the one hand, poverty on the other. When he was ten, Sinclair moved to New York City with his family. Just four years later, he enrolled in the City College of New York, majoring in English literature and supporting himself by selling short stories to popular magazines and comic books.

Upton Sinclair. *Reproduced by permission of AP/Wide World Photos.*

Although he was making a good living, Sinclair grew bored with this kind of writing. In the spring of 1900, when he was twenty-one, he abandoned his thriving career and moved to a cabin in the woods of Quebec, Canada, to focus on his writing. It was in Quebec that Sinclair met his wife, Meta Fuller. Sinclair's first three books were not especially successful, however, and he, his wife, and their infant son suffered from extreme poverty.

In late 1904 a magazine editor suggested to Sinclair that he address the subject of "wage slaves," workers in modern industry, comparing their situation to the slaves in the American South before the Civil War (1861–65). Sinclair had just completed a magazine article about a failed strike in Chicago's meatpacking industry, and he decided to use this as the basis for his next novel. With a five-hundred-dollar advance, he bought a small farm in New Jersey and started to research the book. He spent seven weeks in Chicago, interviewing workers, living among them, and looking at the factories where they worked.

In 1906 Sinclair published this book, titled *The Jungle.* The book exposed the grossly unsanitary conditions under which meat was packaged for consumption and the desperate poverty and dire living conditions forced onto workers in the meatpacking industry. *The Jungle* became an immediate best-seller. The middle-class readers who bought the book demanded government action to ensure the safety of their food supply. President Theodore Roosevelt invited Sinclair to the White House, and shortly afterward pressed Congress to pass legislation for federal inspection of meat. It was an important beginning of government regulation of an industry that had previously yielded huge profits as business owners ignored costly sanitation controls.

According to one biographer, Sinclair once remarked about *The Jungle:* "I aimed at the public's heart, and by accident I hit it in the stomach."

Sinclair continued publishing novels that focused on other social issues of the day, and he chose fiction rather than factual magazine articles as his vehicle to expose the excesses of industrialization. In 1908 he published *The Metropolis,* about New York's high society, and *The Moneychangers,* whose main character was said to resemble American financier **J. P. Morgan** (1837–1913; see entry). *King Coal* (1917), about a coal miners' strike in Colorado in 1913–14 and the brutal living conditions of coal miners was researched and presented in the same manner as *The Jungle*—a book in which facts were presented in the context of fiction. But none of Sinclair's subsequent novels had quite the success, or impact, of *The Jungle.*

Today, *The Jungle* is often remembered as the book that brought about government rules and inspection of packaged food, particularly meat. But for Sinclair, it was a political novel, uncovering great human suffering at the hands of unregulated capitalism (private ownership of goods and property) and focusing on socialism (government owned or regulated business) as the ideal cure for the social ills, such as abuse of workers or unsafe conditions in meatpacking plants, that he documented at the height of the American Industrial Revolution. Socialism was a cause Sinclair continued to support throughout his life, until his death in 1968.

Long after his fellow muckrakers had faded from the political and literary scene, Sinclair continued to campaign against the abuses of the Industrial Revolution. In the 1920s he turned to nonfiction to expose the shortcomings (as he saw it) of American schools. He attacked the integrity and objectivity of journalists, whom he felt were overly influenced by big business. In the late 1920s he wrote sympathetically about the case of Nicola Sacco (1891–1927) and Bartolomeo Vanzetti (1888–1927), Italian-born anarchists (those who reject all forms of government or authority) accused of murder during a robbery near Boston, Massachusetts. Many people believed the evidence against the two men was weak, and that they were really being persecuted for their political beliefs.

In the 1930s Sinclair took an even more direct role in politics. He ran for governor of California in 1933 on a platform that included combating poverty in the state by raising taxes on the film industry centered in Hollywood. The movie studio Metro-Goldwyn-Mayer (MGM) coordinated a campaign to defeat Sinclair, who lost the election.

The last decades of Sinclair's life were spent writing more novels, all with a political tinge to them. In 1967 Sinclair was invited by President Lyndon Johnson (1908–1973) to be present at the signing of the Wholesome Meat Act, a follow-up to the original Meat Inspection and Pure Food and Drug Act that Sinclair's novel had inspired some sixty years earlier.

Upton Sinclair died the next year, on November 25, 1968, in Bound Brook, New Jersey.

Lincoln Steffens, gentleman reporter

Lincoln Steffens was one of the original muckrakers, focusing his attention on the widespread corruption of city officials who were bribed by businesspeople. But over time, Steffens became disillusioned with efforts to reform politics, and concluded that only a revolution, like the ones that took place in Mexico (1910) and Russia (1917), could succeed in defeating the natural tendencies of capitalism toward corruption.

While he became a leading advocate of radical revolutions in the name of the working class, Steffens began life in the lap of luxury. He was born on April 6, 1866, four years after his father had arrived in California by wagon train after the California gold rush had opened the state's natural resources to hordes of immigrants from the East. Steffens's father settled in Sacramento, where he made a modest fortune selling paint. Steffens grew up in one of Sacramento's most stately mansions.

As a boy, Steffens showed signs of the rebelliousness that would mark his entire life. He was a mediocre student who was sent by his parents to a military academy in San Mateo, California, to "straighten out." He enrolled in the University of California at Berkeley, graduating in 1889 with a bachelor's degree in philosophy.

Steffens then launched into a tour of Europe, dabbling in philosophy courses at German universities in Heidelberg, Munich, and Leipzig. He fell in love with Josephine

Bontecou, the daughter of an American physician, while studying in Leipzig and secretly married her in Germany in 1891. The couple moved around Europe for another year, studying in London, England, and Paris, France, and visiting Italy before sailing back to New York. There, the seemingly spoiled young Steffens got a surprise welcome-home present from his father: a check for one hundred dollars, along with a note informing him that he was now on his own.

Steffens became a reporter for the *New York Evening Post* and was assigned to cover the police department, which was in the midst of a corruption scandal. His work put him in touch with an energetic young politician named Theodore Roosevelt, who was soon to become a reform-minded New York City police commissioner (and a few years later, vice president and then president of the United States).

Lincoln Steffens. *Reproduced by permission of the Library of Congress.*

At the end of 1901 Steffens accepted a job offer from S. S. McClure, who had launched *McClure's* magazine. McClure had also hired Ida Tarbell and Ray Stannard Baker (1870–1946), and together with Steffens these writers pushed *McClure's* to the forefront of investigative journalism that came to be called muckraking: exposing corruption and misdeeds by politicians and businessmen throughout the United States.

While Tarbell focused on John D. Rockefeller's Standard Oil Company, Steffens concentrated on the corruption of municipal officials and local business leaders. In October 1902 Steffens published an article on corruption in St. Louis, Missouri, where a crusading local prosecutor was waging a legal war on the bribery of local officials. Steffens followed this story with one on "The Shame of Minneapolis," about corruption in that city's government, which appeared in the same issue of *McClure's* as the first installment of Tarbell's long string of articles about Standard Oil.

Many other writers and publications followed the lead of *McClure's,* but Steffens's stories went beyond just uncovering examples of misdeeds and tried to understand the reasons behind the abuses. In Steffens's view, for example, it was the greed of private businessmen and their desire for special privileges that led them to bribe hapless municipal officials. Steffens's collection of stories about municipal corruption was published in book form as *The Shame of the Cities* in 1904; it became a best-seller.

In 1906 Steffens and several other members of *McClure's* editorial staff who had wearied of the publisher's controlling management of the magazine bought the *American Magazine.* They quickly transformed it into a leading investigative journal, but Steffens left a year later to pursue a freelance career.

In 1911 Steffens's personal life experienced a series of shocks: his wife died, followed shortly thereafter by the death of his mother-in-law, who had lived with him and her daughter. Then both of Steffens's parents died in short succession.

Three years later, Steffens discovered what he thought was a new solution to society's problems: a revolutionary strongman. Steffens's inspiration arose in Mexico, where a revolution, led by Pancho Villa (1878–1923) and Venustiano Carranza (1859–1920), had begun. Steffens went to Mexico to cover the revolution and became persuaded that a strong leader was the path to meaningful reform.

In the spring of 1917 Steffens went to Russia, which experienced two revolutions that year, one in February and a second, the Bolshevik, or Communist, Revolution in November. The revolutions arose in the wake of desperate poverty, indifference on the part of the ruling czar (king), and Russia's long involvement in World War I (1914–18). Steffens interviewed the leaders of the Russian Communists and wrote a sympathetic introduction to a book by Leon Trotsky (1879–1940), one of the revolution's main leaders, in early 1919. It was after an interview with Vladimir Lenin (1870–1924), leader of the new Russian Communist state, that Steffens declared in a letter to a friend: "I have seen the future, and it works." It was a comment widely and often quoted, and one that put Steffens in the communist camp for many years afterward.

Steffens remarried in 1919 and settled in Europe, earning a living by working as a freelance journalist. He traveled to Italy and briefly had praise for the Italian fascist leader Benito Mussolini (1883–1945). But by and large, Steffens had faded from public view.

In 1927 he returned to the United States and lived in Carmel, California. His autobiography was published in 1931, helping to revive his reputation during the deep economic depression that gripped the United States at the time. The book became a best-seller. Suddenly, Steffens was in the spotlight again, writing articles and giving lectures. As the depression continued to bring hardship in the United States, he again advocated the Soviet Union as a model society, where the government had taken over factories and assumed responsibility for citizens' welfare, at least in Steffen's view. Only a few years later did it became known that the Soviet leader, Joseph Stalin (1879–1953), was a brutal dictator who sent millions of citizens to labor camps in Siberia.

Steffens suffered a heart attack in late 1933, and was mostly confined to bed until his death, at home in Carmel, California, on August 9, 1936.

Ida Tarbell and the Standard Oil Company

Ida Tarbell was born in 1857, in a log farm house in Hatch Hollow, Pennsylvania. Two years later in nearby Titusville, Pennsylvania, the world's first oil well was drilled, making northwestern Pennsylvania the center of the country's petroleum industry.

Her father, Franklin Tarbell, had been a farmer and carpenter and turned to manufacturing wooden storage barrels and tanks for the rapidly growing oil industry. It was a successful business, and in time, he joined many others in drilling for oil—an activity that eventually brought him up against the business practices of John D. Rockefeller, who was building the Standard Oil Company. Franklin Tarbell was run out of business by Rockefeller, a fact that played a significant role years later when Franklin's oldest child, Ida, was an established journalist in New York.

Ida was a good student, encouraged by her parents. After graduating high school in Titusville, she enrolled in Allegheny College, a coeducational college sponsored by the

Ida Tarbell. *Reproduced by permission of the Library of Congress.*

Methodist Church in Meadville, Pennsylvania. She was the only woman in the class of 1880. After two years of teaching, Ida instead decided to focus on writing. She returned to Meadville and got an editing job with a monthly magazine called the *Chautauquan,* which was dedicated to self-improvement. The magazine was a success, and so was Ida Tarbell. She worked there for eight years and was promoted to the position of managing editor.

In 1891, when she was thirty-four, Tarbell decided it was time to break out of her comfortable life in western Pennsylvania. She gathered her savings and left for Paris, France, determined to expand her horizons. She lived in the Latin Quarter, an area where many artists lived, and studied at the Sorbonne (University of Paris) and College of Paris. To make a living, she researched people famous in French history and sold articles about them to American magazines. In 1892 she sold an article on Louis Pasteur (1822–1895), the famous French biologist, to *McClure's* magazine. It was the beginning of a long association with *McClure's* that would establish her reputation.

In 1894 Tarbell returned to the United States and became a staff writer for *McClure's.* A series of her articles about President Abraham Lincoln (1809–1865) was later collected as a book, *The Life of Abraham Lincoln,* winning high praise at the time it was published in 1900.

As the new century dawned, the editor of *McClure's* changed its format to put more emphasis on current events and social issues. It was an era when the most successful capitalists, such as John D. Rockefeller and J. P. Morgan, were putting together enormous business enterprises. These trusts (called monopolies today) were powerful enough to drive their competitors out of business. Companies were regularly engaged in bitter, often violent, battles with labor unions trying to organize workers in order to win higher wages and improved working conditions. *McClure's* soon became the most important muckraking publication, focusing on exposing corporate corruption, thievery, and abuses.

Starting in 1902, Tarbell began contributing a series of articles about Rockefeller that eventually stretched over nineteen installments. The pieces were later collected into a two-volume book, *The History of the Standard Oil Company.* By examining thousands of public documents and newspaper articles, Tarbell gradually exposed how Rockefeller had manipulated the oil business into a monopoly called Standard Oil. Tarbell was a skillful writer, capable of tracking the complex story of Rockefeller's dealings in a way that conveyed both the history and a sense of outrage over his unethical business tactics.

The series helped build public sentiment against the company and made it easier for the federal government to sue Standard Oil in federal court for violating the 1890 Sherman Antitrust Act. This act outlawed the practice of a company purchasing other companies for the purpose of eliminating competition in an industry. The suit wound its way through the courts and finally resulted in a Supreme Court decision in 1911. The court ordered that Rockefeller's giant company be broken up into separate, independent—and competing—companies.

In 1906 Tarbell and several of her fellow muckraking journalists left *McClure's* in a group protest over the controlling behavior of its editor and owner. Together, they bought another publication, *American Magazine,* to which Tarbell contributed for another nine years.

Unlike some of her fellow muckrakers, Tarbell continued to believe in the private ownership and control of business. She was enthusiastic about the biggest manufacturer of automobiles, **Henry Ford** (1863–1947; see entry) and his labor policies, which had included raising workers's wages to $5.00 a day in 1914. She later wrote two books full of praise for two businessmen prominent in her time, steel magnate Elbert H. Gary (1846–1927) and Owen D. Young (1874–1962).

Surprisingly to some, for a woman who devoted herself to a career instead of marriage, Tarbell was not a feminist, or even a suffragist (a supporter of women's right to vote, associated with the campaign to pass the Nineteenth Amendment to the U.S. Constitution in 1920). In *The Business of Being a Woman* (1912), she advocated that women should remain at home as mothers, where they could influence their children.

Tarbell retired to her farm in Connecticut, where she died of pneumonia on January 6, 1944.

For More Information

Books

Bloodworth, William A. *Upton Sinclair.* Boston, MA: Twayne Publishers, 1977.

Brady, Kathleen. *Ida Tarbell: Portrait of a Muckraker.* Pittsburgh, PA: University of Pittsburgh Press, 1989.

Camhi, Jane Jerome. *Women against Women: American Anti-Suffragism, 1880–1920.* Brooklyn, NY: Carlson Publications, 1994.

Harris, Leon A. *Upton Sinclair, American Rebel.* New York: Crowell, 1975.

Horton, Russell M. *Lincoln Steffens.* New York: Twayne Publishers, 1974.

Kaplan, Justin. *Lincoln Steffens: A Biography.* New York: Simon and Schuster, 1974.

Kochersberger, Robert C., ed. *More Than a Muckraker: Ida Tarbell's Lifetime in Journalism.* Knoxville, TN: University of Tennessee Press, 1994.

Lane, James B. *Jacob A. Riis and the American City.* Port Washington, NY: Kennikat Press, 1974.

Meyer, Edith Patterson. *"Not Charity, but Justice": The Story of Jacob A. Riis.* New York: Vanguard Press, 1974.

Sinclair, Upton. *Autobiography.* New York: Harcourt, Brace and World, 1962.

Sinclair, Upton. *Boston: A Documentary Novel of the Sacco-Vanzetti Case.* Cambridge, MA: R. Bentley, 1978.

Sinclair, Upton. *The Jungle.* New York: Signet Classics, 2001.

Steffens, Lincoln. *The Autobiography of Lincoln Steffens.* New York: Harcourt, Brace and World, 1968.

Stinson, Robert. *Lincoln Steffens.* New York: F. Ungar Publishing, 1979.

Tarbell, Ida M. *All in the Day's Work: An Autobiography.* Boston, MA: G. K. Hall, 1985.

Tarbell, Ida M. *The Business of Being a Woman.* New York: Macmillan, 1912.

Periodicals

Goldberg, Vicki. "Looking at the Poor in a Gilded Frame: A Series of Recent Photography Shows Suggest Real Concern about Poverty—and a Wish to Deal with It at Arm's Length." *New York Times,* April 9, 1995, p. H1.

Mitchell, Greg. "How Media Politics Was Born: To Keep Upton Sinclair from Becoming Governor of California in 1934, His Opponents Invented a Whole New Kind of Campaign." *American Heritage,* September–October 1988, p. 34.

Reitman, Janet. "The Muckraker vs. the Millionaire." *Scholastic Update,* November 2, 1998, p. 14.

Stein, Harry H. "Apprenticing Reporters: Lincoln Steffens on '*The Evening Post.*'" *Historian,* Winter 1996, p. 367.

Treckel, Paula A. "Lady Muckraker." *American History,* June 2001, p. 38.

Wilson, Christopher. "The Making of a Best Seller, 1906." *New York Times Book Review,* December 22, 1985, p. 1.

Web Sites

"Documentary Photography: Jacob Riis." *Visual Arts Data Service.* http://vads.ahds.ac.uk/vads_catalogue/jrcal_description.html (accessed on February 26, 2003).

"Ida Tarbell: Life and Works." *Ida Tarbell Home Page, Allegheny College.* http://tarbell.alleg.edu/biobib.html (accessed on February 26, 2003).

"The Jacob A. Riis Collection: Selected Images." *Museum of the City of New York.* http://www.mcny.org (accessed on February 26, 2003).

"People and Events: Ida Tarbell, 1857–1944." *PBS American Experience.* http://www.pbs.org/wgbh/amex/rockefellers/peopleevents/p_tarbell.html (accessed on February 26, 2003).

Riis, Jacob. "How the Other Half Lives." *Yale University.* http://www.yale.edu/amstud/inforev/riis/contents.html (accessed on February 26, 2003).

Sinclair, Upton. "End Poverty in California: The EPIC Movement." *Museum of the City of San Francisco.* http://www.sfmuseum.org/hist1/sinclair.html (accessed on February 26, 2003).

Sinclair, Upton. "The Jungle." *Berkeley Digital Library.* http://sunsite.berkeley.edu/Literature/Sinclair/TheJungle/ (accessed on February 26, 2003).

Sinclair, Upton. "Prince Hagen." *Project Gutenberg.* http://ibiblio.org/gutenberg/etext02/prhgn10.txt (accessed on February 26, 2003).

Steffens, Lincoln. "Excerpt from *The Shame of the Cities.*" *History Matters!* http://historymatters.gmu.edu/d/5732/ (accessed on February 26, 2003).

Tarbell, Ida M. "John D. Rockefeller: A Character Study." *Ida Tarbell Home Page, Allegheny College.* http://tarbell.alleg.edu/archives/jdr.html (accessed on February 26, 2003).

Robert Owen

Born May 14, 1771
Newton, Montgomeryshire, Wales

Died November 17, 1858
Newton, Montgomeryshire, Wales

British industrialist

"I know that society may be formed so as to exist without crime, without poverty, with health greatly improved, with little, if any misery, and with intelligence and happiness increased a hundredfold; and no obstacle whatsoever intervenes at this moment except ignorance to prevent such a state of society from becoming universal."

Reproduced by permission of The Library of Congress.

As the owner of a cotton mill, Robert Owen was an early industrialist who envisioned a more humane way of running factories, which he called cooperatives, as well as a system of education for workers. Sometimes called England's first socialist, one who believes in the collective ownership of business, Owen was an idealist (someone who places ideals before practical considerations) who brought his ideas to the United States, but eventually failed to make a permanent mark.

Childhood and youth

Owen was born at Newton, in Montgomeryshire, Wales, in 1771. His father was an ironmonger, someone who sells iron and other hardware, and also served as the town's postmaster. Owen had a reputation as an exceptionally bright student; he was helping teach other children when he was just seven years old, and before he turned ten he had read most of the classics of the day. His father took him out of school when he was ten and arranged for him to become an apprentice (an assistant who is learning a job) in a clothing store in town. Although his formal education did not last long, it proved to be sufficient for Owen to succeed in business later in life.

Owen eventually made his way to Manchester, England, in 1786 just as the Industrial Revolution, a period of rapid economic change that began in Great Britain in the middle of the eighteenth century, was starting to have an enormous impact on the textile industry. The industry, made up of companies involved in the production of yarn and cloth, was rapidly changing as the result of new technology. Newly invented machines enabled fewer workers to produce more yarn, or cloth, than ever before. Textile workers who once worked independently at home found themselves employed in factories where the large and expensive new machines were housed and operated. People who previously worked for themselves became paid employees of the owners of the new machines.

The beginning of his life's work

Owen was fifteen when he arrived in Manchester, England, and his success came early. He met a young engineer named Ernest Jones, and in 1789, believing that the new machines were the future of the textile industry, Owen borrowed £100 (a little more than $160) from his brother and went into business manufacturing a yarn-making machine called a spinning mule, used to manufacture yarn from cotton or wool fibers. Owen ran the business while Jones oversaw the machinery.

Jones did not stay with the business long, and Owen continued with just three employees. Owen earned a good reputation in Manchester, and in 1792 he was hired to manage a large spinning factory, Chorton Twist, owned by Peter Drinkwater. Owen, now twenty-two years old, was supervising five hundred employees at a modern steam-powered mill. Chorton Twist rapidly expanded under Owen's management and became well known for its high-quality cotton yarn. Owen was eventually made a partner in the company.

Owen's interests went well beyond managing a factory. In 1792 he had been invited to join the Manchester Literary and Philosophical Society. The group held meetings at which members gave lectures and debated issues of the day. Among the members were the poet Samuel Taylor Coleridge (1772–1834) and public health pioneer Dr. Thomas Percival (1740–1804). Owen was active in the society and presented his own papers on subjects such as "The Improvement of the Cotton Industry" and "Universal Happiness and Industrialization."

Owen's position at Chorton Twist led him to meet many businesspeople in the thriving textile industry, including David Dale (1739–1806), who owned four factories in New Lanark, Scotland. Owen became close friends with Dale, and especially with Dale's daughter, Caroline, whom he married in 1799. Soon thereafter, Owen raised £60,000 (more than $97,000) from several businessmen in Manchester and bought his father-in-law's share in the company.

New Lanark

The factories in New Lanark, Scotland, employed almost two thousand people, including five hundred children who had been sent from orphanages. In situations like this, which were not uncommon at the time, factory owners were responsible for housing, feeding, and clothing these young workers. The result was that many grew up without an education, ill-fed and ill-clothed. Even worse, many were injured, maimed, or killed outright, in industrial accidents.

In some respects, the conditions of the adult workers were not much better. They worked long hours in dark mills for little pay. Abuse of alcohol was a problem among the men, who sometimes drank to relieve their despair.

Owen's first claim to historical fame was to recognize that the poor habits of workers, including drunkenness, might reflect their working conditions rather than be a sign of a defect in their characters. Almost uniquely among mill owners, Owen resolved to improve the conditions of his employees.

He gained his workers' trust in 1806, when he continued to pay them for four months while his factory was shut down because of a ban on cotton exports imposed by the United States in a dispute with the British government. (Owen used American cotton to spin yarn.) Then he attempted to shorten the working day, from thirteen hours to twelve.

But pressure from his business partners to increase profits actually forced him to increase the workday, to fourteen hours, at least temporarily. (He finally introduced the twelve-hour day in 1816). But in other areas, he had more success.

Owen greatly improved the housing his company provided to workers and paved the surrounding streets, which he paid to keep clean. He opened a company store to sell food and other merchandise to workers, and used profits from the store to fund a community school. Children from age two to six attended the Infant School, then graduated to the day school until age ten when they started working in the factory. But children could still attend the night school that Owen set up.

Owen believed that education should go beyond basic reading, writing and arithmetic in order to build good character and encourage good behavior throughout life. He was a pioneer in what today would be called a liberal education, as well as in modern education techniques. His schools introduced music, dancing, and games to schools, and pictures, maps, and charts were used to help students learn. Previously school consisted entirely of printed books that taught the basics. Owen had the idea that education could be fun and natural—a radical departure from what was generally practiced in his day.

Owen did not allow corporal punishment (spanking, for example) and insisted that teachers treat students with kindness. Instruction was to be by conversation, rather than one-way lectures, and lessons should alternate with play. Children were encouraged to think and act rationally.

In 1816 he opened the Institute for the Formation of Character near his factories, extending his educational ideas to adult workers. In the same rooms where young children attended classes in the daytime, adults could attend lectures and concerts at night. Owen also took an interest in the morality of his employees. On his mill's property, a form of local government was organized, which imposed fines for drunkenness. Owen paid supervisors to keep track of the behavior of workers; a black mark was recorded for instances of bad behavior, a white mark for good behavior, with blue and yellow marks for behaviors in between. Although Owen noted some improvement in the lives of his workers, his experiment did not spread to other factories.

Overall, Owen's ideas were widely praised but seldom adopted by others. His business partners strongly objected to the methods employed, partly on grounds of cost and partly on grounds of their own ideas about morality. Gradually the music and dancing stopped (some of his partners, members of the Society of Friends, or Quakers, objected on religious grounds), and formal religious education was introduced. By 1824, pressure from his partners forced Owen to end his connection with the school at New Lanark, fifteen years after he had started.

Taking reform to the masses

As early as 1802, some British politicians had advocated the sort of reforms on a national basis that Owen tried to introduce in his factory, such as a limit on the length of the workday, a minimum age for working long hours, and education for children (who often worked in factories as early as age six). Initially led by Robert Peel (1750–1830), himself a textile businessman and father of the future British prime minister, also named Robert Peel (1788–1850), these initiatives were introduced as bills (proposed laws) in Parliament. Owen was called as a witness in favor of such reforms, and he even drafted proposals for new laws himself. But opposition by other business owners to any government interference in their businesses was strong, and it was not until 1819 that a watered-down version of Owen's factory reform bill was made law. It took another fourteen years to pass a law requiring inspection of factories to make sure the regulations were enforced.

Discouraged by the work of Parliament, Owen decided to appeal directly to the public. He published his ideas in a book titled *New View of Society,* in which he outlined his ideas for a system run on a cooperative basis. Instead of bosses and owners, Owen proposed an arrangement in which everyone at a factory would jointly own and operate the business, with democratic votes on key decisions. He based his work on the reforms introduced at New Lanark, which had been highly successful. To solve the problem of unemployment, for example, which was plaguing Britain and leading to widespread poverty and rioting, Owen proposed organizing new cooperatives that could operate along the lines of his own factory.

While some people liked Owen's ideas about treating workers as partners and assuring them a decent living, others strongly objected to his ideas about religion. Owen strongly believed in the power of science to explain natural phenomena, and insisted that people should not believe in ideas that could not be demonstrated and proved by science. In his book *A New View of Society,* Owen advocated setting up schools independent of the Church of England (most English schools were run by the church in Owen's era) in order to encourage children to think rationally without confusing scientific studies and religious teachings. Owen's criticisms of the official Church of England annoyed church officials and eventually some of Owen's supporters (but not Owen himself) were accused of the crime of blasphemy (showing contempt or irreverence toward God). Eventually Owen financed buildings he called Halls of Science, which promoted his social ideals without including religious elements that were not based on science.

New Harmony, Indiana

In 1824 Owen learned that a religious sect (group) in Indiana that had organized their own community, called New Harmony, wanted to sell their property. Here, he thought, was an opportunity to buy an entire town and set up a utopia (a place where things are perfect) by implementing his ideas for an ideal society without meddling by a Parliament, church, or edgy business partners. In fact, his ideas seemed welcome in the United States, and he was even invited to address the U.S. Congress.

Owen acquired the New Harmony settlement for $125,000 and set forth on a project to prove that his ideas could work. He recruited new settlers to come to the town and run agricultural and small industrial ventures on the principles of a cooperative (see box on page 136). While he was traveling, his son William was left in charge of the settlement.

Things did not go smoothly at New Harmony. Settlers flocked there, but many were not suited for the sort of social experiment Owen had in mind. Some newcomers lacked practical skills to run a farm or a factory, and instead of contributing to the enterprise actually became a drain. William urged his father to stop sending new inhabitants, as the town became overcrowded. With constant supervision by Robert Owen, the community managed to run relatively smoothly, but the minute he was absent, dissatisfaction grew. The community split into different groups, some restricting their cooperative spirit to religion, education, or recreation. Owen's ideal of cooperative business ventures faltered.

By 1828, four years after he started the venture, Owen handed New Harmony over to his sons and went back to England. For him, the experiment at New Harmony was over.

What Is a Cooperative?

A cooperative is a group of people, sometimes living in a community or sometimes just working for an enterprise, who agree to work for the common good. They tend to contribute to the community or business as best they can, and everyone shares alike in the results.

The idea of a cooperative was shocking to many people in Robert Owen's social class, who were used to receiving much more income than workers. It was more appealing to workers, and to revolutionaries who emerged during the Industrial Revolution, including **Karl Marx** (1818–1883; see entry). Marx, the father of modern communism, advocated an end result that was similar to Owen's ideal, but thought that a violent revolution by workers against business owners was the only away to achieve such a society.

Robert Owen, organizer

Owen had sold his interest in the factories at New Lanark to finance New Harmony, and the failed cooperative left him without much money. But he found that British workers appreciated his ideas about improving their welfare, even if the upper and middle class of Britain did not. Workers were beginning to form trade unions—organizations in which workers joined together to demand better wages and working conditions from their employers—as a means of achieving the benefits advocated by Owen, such as limited work hours and an end to employment of young children.

Still spurred by strong idealism, Owen plunged into the union movement. He opened a newspaper, and then the National Equitable Labor Exchange in London, a place where people could acquire goods in exchange for work or for things they had produced. Workers paid in notes, like currency, which represented the number of hours worked and which could be exchanged for other goods worth a comparable number of hours.

In 1832, Owen suggested that trade unions, which typically represented workers in a particular industry or occupation, should unite. Two years later, the Grand National Consolidated Trade Union was formed in Britain. It had half a million members within a week, which alarmed the government. But the new union did not last long in the face of opposition by employers. Strikes by workers (refusal to work until union demands were met) and lockouts by employers (in which an employer fights union demands by shutting a factory and refusing to pay workers) caused the Grand National Consolidated Trade Union to collapse shortly after it was organized. Lack of funds forced Owen to close his newspaper and his labor exchange.

After 1835 Owen lived modestly, still actively promoting his "new view of society" through books and pamphlets. His followers, known as Owenites, held meetings around England to promote his ideals, but ultimately, none of the organizations or causes he supported managed to attract enough support to succeed. In 1858, Owen fell ill and asked to be taken to his birthplace of Newton, where he died on November 17, 1858. At his request, he was buried next to his parents in a churchyard cemetery.

For More Information

Books

Harrison, J. F. C. *Quest for the New Moral World: Robert Owen and the Owenites in Britain and America.* New York: Scribner's, 1969.

Jones, Lloyd. *The Life, Times, and Labours of Robert Owen.* New York: AMS Press, 1971.

Owen, Robert. *A New View of Society and Other Writings.* New York: Penguin Books, 1991.

Pollard, Sidney, and John Salt, eds. *Robert Owen, Prophet of the Poor: Essays in Honour of the Two Hundredth Anniversary of His Birth.* London, England: Macmillan, 1971.

Sargant, William Lucas. *Robert Owen and His Social Philosophy.* New York: AMS Press, 1971.

Periodicals

Barker, Paul. "In New Lanark Robert Owen Tried to Forge a New Society. Today, His Model Village Is a Visitor Centre." *New Statesman,* August 7, 1998, p. 54.

Cowell, Alan. "Britain's 'Satanic Mills' Now a Valued Heritage." *New York Times,* February 10, 2002.

Web Sites

Gordon, Peter. "Robert Owen (1771–1858)." http://www.ibe.unesco.org/International/Publications/Thinkers/ ThinkersPdf/owene.PDF (accessed on March 3, 2003).

"Owen, Robert." *Encyclopedia of Marxism.* http://www.marxists.org/glossary/people/o/w.htm#owen (accessed on February 13, 2003).

Owen, Robert. "A New View of Society." *Avalon Project at Yale Law School.* http://www.yale.edu/lawweb/avalon/econ/owenm.htm (accessed on February 13, 2003).

Robert Owen Museum. http://robert-owen.midwales.com (accessed on February 13, 2003).

"Robert Owen, 1771–1858." *History of Economic Thought.* http://cepa.newschool.edu/het/profiles/owen.htm (accessed on March 25, 2003).

John D. Rockefeller

Born July 8, 1839
Richford, New York

Died May 23, 1937
Ormond Beach, Florida

American businessman, philanthropist

John D. Rockefeller built his fortune in the oil business from the ground up. His phenomenally successful Standard Oil Company dominated the oil industry for nearly forty years and became one of the first big trusts (monopolies) in the United States. The federal government, under President **Theodore Roosevelt** (1858–1919; see entry), attacked the Standard Oil Trust in court, and succeeded in forcing it to split into separate companies in order to stimulate competition.

When Rockefeller died just six weeks short of his ninety-eighth birthday, he was thought to have amassed a personal fortune worth $5 billion (about $50 billion in 2002 prices). Increasingly throughout his life, his interests turned to philanthropy (goodwill to fellow people, especially the active effort to promote human welfare), donating half a billion dollars to fund universities and medical research, among other things. The influence of his philanthropic institutions has continued to grow after his death.

"I know of nothing more despicable and pathetic than a man who devotes all the hours of the waking day to the making of money for money's sake."

Reproduced by permission of Getty Images.

Childhood and youth

John Davison Rockefeller was not born into wealth. He was born on a farm near the small town of Richford, in the middle of New York State, the second of six children born to William and Eliza Rockefeller. One writer describes Rockefeller's father as a "snake oil salesman," a dealer in ineffective substances or mixtures promoted as having medicinal value. The family moved several times before Rockefeller was a teenager. In 1853, when he was fourteen, the family bought a house in Strongsville, Ohio, near Cleveland.

Rockefeller attended Central High School in Cleveland, renting a room in the city so that he could be closer to school. He also joined the Erie Street Baptist Church. Young Rockefeller became a trustee of his church at age twenty-one, and was strongly religious for the rest of his life. For many years, he taught Sunday school and served on church boards with streetcar conductors and other working-class people. He also took seriously the religious conviction to give away one-tenth of what he earned, even when starting out at a very low salary.

Rockefeller did not graduate from high school. Instead, he left Central High to attend the Folsom Mercantile College, where he spent three months completing a course in accounting. In 1855 he was hired as an assistant bookkeeper at Hewitt and Tuttle, a small wholesale grocery company. It was three months before he received his first paycheck—for $50, or about $3.50 a week. He soon received a raise to $6.25 a week. (These figures reflect the value of a dollar in 1855; in 2002, Rockefeller's weekly salary would have been worth about $120.) A few months after that, he was promoted to cashier and head bookkeeper.

Meet Mrs. Rockefeller

In 1864 Rockefeller married Laura Celestia Spelman (1839–1915), who had been a classmate of his at Central High School. Laura was a school teacher and the daughter of a successful Cleveland businessman. The Rockefellers had five children, one of whom died as an infant.

Initially the family lived on Euclid Avenue in Cleveland. In later years, as Rockefeller's oil business grew, he

John D. Rockefeller and four associates built an oil refinery in Cleveland, Ohio, in 1863, just a few years after oil was discovered in the nearby town of Titusville, Pennsylvania. *Reproduced by permission of the Corbis Corporation.*

bought a house in New York City (on West Fifty-fourth Street, where the Museum of Modern Art is now located). Rockefeller also bought a country estate at Pocantico Hills, north of New York City, as well as country estates in Lakewood, New Jersey, and Ormond Beach, Florida. Despite the many residences, Rockefeller lived simply, had few pleasures, and was devoted to his family

Getting started

Rockefeller spent four years working for Hewitt and Tuttle. In that time, he managed to save one thousand dollars. In 1859 he took his savings, borrowed another thousand dollars from his father, and launched his own grocery business. That same year, in Titusville, Pennsylvania, a few miles almost directly east of Cleveland, the first American oil well was drilled. It was a discovery of enormous significance to the Industrial Revolution, a period of fast-paced economic change that began in Great Britain in the middle of the eighteenth century, and certainly to Rockefeller.

Four years after starting their grocery business, Rockefeller and his business partner Maurice Clark decided to get into the oil business. Cleveland had become a center of oil refining, and after taking on a third partner, Samuel Andrews, Rockefeller and Clark built an oil refinery while continuing their grocery business.

In 1865 there was a disagreement among the group's partners, which by now numbered five, and they agreed to sell their oil refinery to Rockefeller. He sold the rest of his interest in the grocery business and, with Samuel Andrews as his sole remaining partner, launched the oil refining business of Rockefeller and Andrews.

Gaining momentum

Petroleum played a key role in the development of the Industrial Revolution. It was especially useful in transportation, since liquid petroleum products (such as gasoline and diesel fuel) were easier to use than coal. The development of a practical internal combustion engine (1885) and diesel engine (1892), both needing gasoline to run, soon made petroleum a key factor in transportation.

Initially, though, kerosene was the major product that Rockefeller produced. Kerosene was widely used to fuel lamps in residential houses, in place of candles, and Rockefeller and Andrews's refining business grew rapidly. (The Edison light bulb did not come along until 1879, and even then it was many years before electricity achieved widespread distribution.)

In 1870, eleven years after the formation of Rockefeller and Andrews, the two organized a new company with some additional partners, including Rockefeller's brother, William Rockefeller, Henry M. Flagler, and S. V. Harkness. The new partnership invested $1 million (compared with the $72,000 Rockefeller paid to obtain the first refinery five years earlier) in the new venture; its name was the Standard Oil Company.

Within two years, Standard Oil had bought up almost all the other refineries in Cleveland, as well as two near New

Elements of the Oil Business

- **Drilling.** Oil exists in large underground pools, or reservoirs. Drilling is the process of getting the oil out of the ground by sinking a well into the reservoir. Sometimes oil comes gushing up through the well; other times, it has to be pumped, especially after the reservoir has been tapped for a while. The advantage of the drilling business is that the oil itself costs nothing. There is a cost of drilling a well, however, and if no oil is found, the money is lost. If oil is found, often the owner of the land gets a share.

- **Transportation.** When John D. Rockefeller first got into the business, oil was usually stored in wooden barrels and shipped by wagon, or later by rail, to refineries where it could be turned into useful products. Refined products, such as kerosene, gasoline, and diesel fuel, also have to be distributed from the refinery to customers (at gasoline stations, for example).

- **Refining.** Before it can be used, the crude oil that comes from the ground must be refined. Oil from the ground is often black and thick, whereas a refined product, like gasoline or kerosene, is usually clear and much thinner. The chemical process of extracting molecules of hydrocarbons (those containing a combination of hydrogen and carbon atoms) that can be converted into energy is called refining. This is the part of the oil business that John D. Rockefeller entered.

- **Distribution.** After crude oil has been refined into various products, it must be distributed to customers. This involves transportation, again, and outlets for selling at retail, such as a gasoline station.

York. The company was refining almost thirty thousand barrels of crude oil a day. It even manufactured its own wooden barrels and owned plants that manufactured paint and glue, byproducts of oil refining.

In 1882 Standard Oil and all of its properties were merged into the Standard Oil Trust, with forty-two owners and a value of $70 million (worth about $1.15 billion in 2002 dollars).

In 1892 a state court in Ohio ruled that the Standard Oil Trust violated state law and ordered it to be broken up.

What Is a Trust and Why Is It Illegal?

In 1882 John D. Rockefeller renamed his company Standard Oil Trust, and in 1906 the federal government sued the company for violating the 1890 Sherman Antitrust Act. What was the controversy about?

A trust is a combination of corporations that operate as one and has a monopoly (control) over an industry. In 1890 the U.S. Congress outlawed trusts, because of their ability to control prices and to drive out of business companies attempting to compete in the same industry. The "free enterprise" economic system long embraced by the United States is based on the idea that competition results in the lowest prices and greatest innovation, which benefits consumers. (The opposing idea, socialism, holds that the government should regulate economic activity to achieve the best results.)

Antitrust laws recognize that in some circumstances, such as when one company controls the majority of the market, there is no "free" competition since the big company can (and does) take actions that make it impossible for smaller competitors to remain in business.

Rockefeller quickly moved to form a new company, Standard Oil Company (New Jersey), under a law passed in New Jersey that made such arrangements legal.

Giving it away

Rockefeller was president of Standard Oil until 1911, the same year that the U.S. Supreme Court ruled that Standard Oil violated the 1890 Sherman Antitrust Act and ordered the company broken up into thirty-eight separate companies. But it was fifteen years before then that Rockefeller retired and, at age fifty-seven, turned his attention to a second career: philanthropy, or the promoting of human welfare, especially by donating money to worthy causes. At the time of his retirement, Rockefeller owned about one-fourth of the shares in Standard Oil, as well as extensive holdings in mines, timberland, and other manufacturing and transportation companies.

The importance of donating money to worthy causes was not something new in Rockefeller's life. Since his earliest

By the turn of the twentieth century, Standard Oil controlled about 90 percent of the oil-refining business in the United States, and the Sherman Antitrust Act of 1890 was actually passed with Rockefeller's Standard Oil in mind. The act outlaws contracts and conspiracies designed to eliminate competition, and it prohibits monopolies or attempts to create a monopoly. Specific activities outlawed include: charging prices below what it costs to make a product, so that competitors are driven out of business (or decide not to get into the business in the first place); or entering secret deals with other companies, even in different businesses, so that competitors are driven out of business (for example, getting freight rates lower than are available elsewhere). Since the Sherman Antitrust Act was passed, the federal government has found it difficult to prove that large companies have engaged in illegal practices designed to create anticompetitive monopolies, or trusts.

days in Cleveland, Ohio, he had given 10 percent of his income to his church. As a wealthy businessman, he was known for distributing dimes (worth about a dollar at 2002 prices) to children who came up to him on the street. But Rockefeller's philanthropy was more serious than giving away coins. Funding from his vast fortune helped create or support institutions that have long outlived their benefactor. Among them are:

- **The University of Chicago.** In 1889 Rockefeller contributed $600,000 toward the founding of the University of Chicago, a project of the American Baptist Education Society. It was often Rockefeller's practice to contribute part of the money needed for a project as a means of encouraging others to make contributions as well. The University of Chicago was incorporated in 1890 and subsequently received many other Rockefeller gifts totaling $35 million by 1910 (roughly $600 million at 2002 prices).

- **The Rockefeller Institute for Medical Research (now called Rockefeller University).** Rockefeller founded the institute in order to discover how to prevent and cure diseases. The institute, located in New York City, has been a leader in medical research and can claim credit for such achievements as the treatment of infantile paralysis, spinal meningitis, pneumonia, and the identification of DNA in genetics.

- **The General Education Board.** Rockefeller established and funded the General Education Board in 1902 to improve education, especially for the benefit of medical schools. The board distributed $325 million between 1902 and 1965, when it was dissolved.

- **The Rockefeller Foundation.** The Rockefeller Foundation was established in 1913 to "promote the well-being of mankind throughout the world." As with other Rockefeller philanthropic ventures, the Rockefeller Foundation often concentrated on health projects, especially in areas of public health and medical education. The foundation funded projects that addressed many diseases found in underdeveloped countries, such as malaria and yellow fever. The foundation continues to fund research in agriculture, as well as nonmedical projects.

Throughout his life Rockefeller also made generous contributions to the Baptist Church, the Young Men' Christian Association (YMCA) and the Young Women's Christian Association (YWCA), and the Anti-Saloon League, as befitting a serious, straitlaced teetotaler (one who does not drink alcoholic beverages).

Rockefeller died in Ormond Beach, Florida, on May 23, 1937, at the age of ninety-seven. He was buried in Cleveland, Ohio, in Lakeview Cemetery, having left a legacy both as one of the original monopolists and one of the most generous philanthropists in American history.

For More Information

Books

Abels, Jules. *The Rockefeller Billions: The Story of the World's Most Stupendous Fortune.* New York: Macmillan, 1965.

Chernow, Ron. *Titan: The Life of John D. Rockefeller, Sr.* New York: Random House, 1998.

Coffey, Ellen Greenman. *John D. Rockefeller, Empire Builder.* Englewood Cliffs, NJ: Silver Burdett, 1989.

Myers, Elisabeth P. *John D. Rockefeller, Boy Financier.* Indianapolis, IN: Bobbs-Merrill, 1973.

Periodicals

Birmingham, Stephen. "Our Celebrated Eccentrics." *Harper's Bazaar,* October 1982, p. 88.

Chernow, Ron. "Blessed Barons." *Time,* December 7, 1998, p. 74.

Loomis, Carol J. "The Rockefellers: End of a Dynasty?" *Fortune,* August 4, 1986, p. 26.

Web Sites

"John D. Rockefeller, 1839–1937." *Rockefeller University.* http://www.rockefeller.edu/archive.ctr/jdrsrbio.html (accessed on February 14, 2003).

"The Rockefellers." *PBS American Experience.* http://www.pbs.org/wgbh/amex/rockefellers/index.html (accessed on February 14, 2003).

Tarbell, Ida M. "John D. Rockefeller, a Character Study." *Ida Tarbell Home Page, Allegheny College.* http://tarbell.alleg.edu/archives/jdr.html (accessed on February 14, 2003).

Theodore Roosevelt

Born October 27, 1858
New York, New York

Died January 6, 1919
Oyster Bay, New York

American politician

"The things that will destroy America are prosperity-at-any-price, peace-at-any-price, safety-first instead of duty-first, the love of soft living, and the get-rich-quick theory of life."

Reproduced by permission of the Library of Congress.

Theodore Roosevelt was the twenty-sixth president of the United States, serving from 1901 (after the assassination of President William McKinley [1843–1901]) until 1909. An extraordinary individual by any measure, Roosevelt took strong action to curb the powers of so-called corporate trusts, or monopolies, that had been built up as the Industrial Revolution blossomed in the last decade of the nineteenth century. In so doing, Roosevelt set the precedent for modern government regulation of business.

Before he was president, Roosevelt had been a deputy sheriff in North Dakota and a war hero who led his men into withering enemy fire during a cavalry charge in the Battle of San Juan Hill, in Cuba, during the Spanish-American War (1898). During a campaign for a third term in office, he was wounded in the chest in an assassination attempt, but insisted on delivering his speech despite spitting up blood. He was widely admired as an author of history and wildlife books and as a leading conservationist. And it was Roosevelt who harnessed his extraordinary energy and spirit to go after the giant corporations that, in his view, threatened competition in the first decade of the twentieth century.

Roosevelt was a contemporary of such giants of the Industrial Revolution as **J. P. Morgan** (1837–1913) and **John D. Rockefeller** (1839–1937; see entries) in an era when wealthy business owners were trying to build trusts, or effective monopolies, over such key industries as railroads and petroleum. Roosevelt believed that trusts stifled competition and did not benefit the United States, and he took an aggressive stand to break them up and restore competition.

Moreover, Roosevelt was the first president to establish agencies to protect public health by insisting on federal meat inspection, for instance, in the wake of revelations of horrific violations of basic sanitation in slaughterhouses. He also campaigned for an income tax, a federal minimum wage, and an eight-hour work day. A century after he took office, Theodore Roosevelt was still ranked among the half-dozen most-admired presidents.

Birth, childhood and early career

Theodore Roosevelt was born into a wealthy, long-established family in New York City in 1858, less than three years before the outbreak of the U.S. Civil War (1861–65). His ancestors had come to New York when it was still the Dutch colony of New Amsterdam, in the 1640s. His mother, Martha Bulloch, was a descendant of the first president of the Georgia provincial legislature. Theodore (also called "Teddy") grew up in a cultured house in Manhattan, a member of New York City's aristocracy.

He was educated by private tutors. As a boy, Roosevelt suffered from asthma and poor eyesight and was regarded as somewhat weak and sickly. Legend has it that one day when he was around eleven, his father told him, "You have the mind but not the body and without the help of the body the mind cannot go as far as it should. You must make your body." And so he did. Using a punching bag and lifting weights in an exercise room his father installed in their townhouse, Roosevelt built up his body. When he was fourteen, he was beaten by a bully, and thereafter took boxing and wrestling lessons, and eventually learned the Asian art of self-defense called jujitsu.

Roosevelt learned his lessons well. Later, after he had been elected to the New York State legislature, he once knocked a political opponent unconscious. Before that, living as a rancher in the Dakotas where he worked as a deputy sheriff, he slammed a wanted man to a saloon floor. Even as president, he threw the governor of New Mexico down a flight of stairs during a reunion of the Rough Riders, his old regiment from the Spanish-American War.

Roosevelt grew up just at the time the United States was becoming fully engrossed in the Industrial Revolution, a period marked by the widespread replacement of manual labor by machines that began in Great Britain in the middle of the eighteenth century, and in the half-century when European settlers were heading west in wagon trains or via the new railroads that were being built. He reflected the spirit of *machismo* (pronounced ma-CHEESE-moe, from a Spanish word referring to masculine pride) associated with the American cowboy.

Roosevelt attended Harvard University, where he earned academic honors. He considered a career as a naturalist but disliked Harvard's concentration on laboratory work instead of studies outdoors in the field. His father died suddenly in 1878, when he was halfway through Harvard, and he considered becoming a lawyer after graduating in 1880. But eager to pursue his interests in history and politics, he dropped out of Columbia University's law school.

In 1882 Roosevelt decided to write a history of the War of 1812, one of more than fifty books he eventually authored. That same year, a Republican Party leader in New York recruited Roosevelt to run for the New York State legislature. Roosevelt won the seat and served in the Albany legislature for three terms, receiving positive notices in the press. Among other causes, Roosevelt worked to root out corruption in the New York City government and supported laws favoring the rights of working people.

Roosevelt married Alice Hathaway Lee of Chestnut Hill, Massachusetts, in 1880. In February 1884 his wife died not long after the birth of their daughter, Alice Lee; Roosevelt's mother died the same day. Grief stricken, Roosevelt retreated to a ranch he had bought in Dakota Territory, where he lived the strenuous life of a cowboy and occasional deputy sheriff.

Theodore Roosevelt (center) gained nationwide acclaim by leading a cavalry charge during the Battle of San Juan Hill, in Cuba, during the Spanish-American War. His fame as leader of the Rough Riders (pictured) led to his rapid political ascent. *Reproduced by permission of the National Archives and Records Administration.*

Back to politics

Two years later, Roosevelt returned to the East Coast and reentered politics, while at the same time turning out a series of history volumes. He ran unsuccessfully for mayor of New York in 1886, and two years later supported the successful Republican ticket that installed Benjamin Harrison (1833–1901) as president. In return for Roosevelt's political support, Harrison named him a civil service commissioner in 1889, in charge of regulating the hiring of federal employees. In this job, as in other political jobs he held, Roosevelt was determined to fight corruption. He soon earned a reputation as an honest reformer.

Partly as a result of this image, Roosevelt was appointed police commissioner of New York City in 1895, a job that enhanced his reputation for fighting corruption. After Republican William McKinley (1843–1901) was elected president in 1896, Roosevelt was named assistant secretary of the navy; in this post he became a strong advocate for going to war against Spain in order to control Cuba, Puerto Rico, and the Philippines. When war did break out, Roosevelt insisted on resigning his post and organizing a cavalry group (soldiers trained to fight on horseback) to fight in Cuba. Known as the Rough Riders, the regiment earned fame, and Roosevelt became a national hero by leading his men in a charge into merciless gunfire in the Battle of San Juan Hill in 1898.

As a returning war hero Roosevelt made an attractive candidate for vice president on the Republican ticket headed by President McKinley in 1900. Not everyone was happy with McKinley's choice; some Republican politicians were uncomfortable having a man with Roosevelt's personality in line to become president. And in September 1901, their fears were realized when McKinley was shot at the world's fair in Buffalo, New York. President McKinley died a few days later, and Roosevelt, at age forty-three, became president.

Peace in the coal mines

Roosevelt was president for slightly more than seven years, the remaining three and a half years of McKinley's term and a full term that he won in his own right in the election of 1904. In a sense, his was the first presidency of the twentieth century, and much attention was focused on Roosevelt's foreign policy, summarized in the African proverb he occasionally quoted: "Speak softly, and carry a big stick." Under Roosevelt's leadership, the United States assumed a position as an equal to the main European powers in an era when African, Asian, and Latin American countries were largely dominated by European economic and military power.

Inside the United States, the Roosevelt administration defined a new relationship between government and private business as the Industrial Revolution overwhelmed the older agricultural economy of the United States. Two economic issues dominated the Roosevelt administration: the unrestricted power of monopolies (called trusts) and the emergence of workers as an organized political force.

Up until the Roosevelt administration, the U.S. government had played a small role in economic affairs. The prevailing philosophy was that business could, and should, look

Theodore Roosevelt was one of the most remarkable personalities ever to occupy the White House, possessed by seemingly boundless intellectual and physical energy. *Reproduced by permission of Getty Images.*

after its own affairs, and the government should leave the economy to business leaders. The only role for government, it was thought by some, was to protect property rights and public order, which sometimes included suppressing workers trying to organize strikes. Of course, labor organizers had long been trying to organize unions (organizations of workers devoted to obtaining higher pay and better working conditions), and socialists (people who believe in government control over the economy) had long advocated democratic, government control over big business.

Under Roosevelt, a new role emerged for government: looking out for the good of the ordinary citizen and countering the power of private corporations—a role that government continues to take in the twenty-first century.

Roosevelt's first economic crisis came in 1902. Coal miners in Pennsylvania went on strike to demand higher wages, an eight-hour (as opposed to twelve-hour) workday, and recognition of their union, the United Mine Workers of America. The shutdown of the coal mines threatened to shut down the railroads as well, to close industries dependent on coal for fuel, and also to deprive millions of Americans in the Northeast of fuel to heat their homes in the coming winter.

For the mine owners, the issue was not just economic, but one of prestige as well. They resisted recognizing the union's role in coal mining and demanded that the federal government dispatch troops to end the strike. The strike had been accompanied by violence on both sides, resulting in several deaths. The two sides were unable to reach an agreement.

According to historian Edmund Morris, the governor of Massachusetts warned Roosevelt: "Unless you end this strike, the workers in the North will begin tearing down buildings for fuel. They will not stand being frozen to death."

Roosevelt faced a dilemma. As he noted at the time: "Unfortunately the strength of my public position before the country is also its weakness. I am genuinely independent of the big monied men in all matters where I think the interests of the public are concerned, and probably I am the first President of recent times of whom this could truthfully be said."

Eventually Roosevelt settled on a suggestion by the governor of Massachusetts, W. Murray Crane: a government arbitration panel would be set up to examine the issues separating the miners and the mine owners and recommend a compromise. Roosevelt sent a telegram to seven leading mine owners and to the mineworkers' union, inviting them to a conference in Washington, D.C., on October 3, 1902.

At the conference, Roosevelt told the owners and the union that there were in fact three parties to their dispute: the mine owners, the miners, and the public, represented by

Roosevelt himself. Initially the mine owners refused Roosevelt's suggestion to settle the dispute. They apparently believed that their property rights were being threatened and arrogantly stalked out of a meeting with Roosevelt, insisting that he send in federal troops to guard their mines against the union and protect strikebreaking workers willing to go back to work.

Facing a potential national crisis, Roosevelt told the mine owners that he was prepared to use federal troops—not to end the strike by forcing strikers back to work, as the owners wanted, but to seize the mines from the owners and get coal supplies flowing again.

Ten days after the president first convened the meeting between mine owners and the union, the owners made a major concession: they would accept arbitration (referring a dispute to an impartial group for judgement on the matter), and they would accept the United Mine Workers union as the representative of their workers. The crisis was over. Eventually, both the miners and mine owners accepted the compromise settlement proposed by Roosevelt's commission. The big winner was the president, whose popularity soared as the crisis over winter heating disappeared. According to Sean McCollum, he later wrote about the settlement in a letter to his sister:

> The little world in which the [mine owners] moved was absolutely out of touch with the big world that included practically all the rest of the country.... The trouble with those who said that they would rather die of cold than yield on such a high principle as recognizing arbitration with these miners was that they were not in danger of dying of cold ... but the poor people around them could not get coal and with them it would not be discomfort but acute misery and loss of life.

Roosevelt's successful strategy set the precedent for presidential involvement in labor disputes thereafter.

Busting the trusts

Roosevelt's other great economic challenge came from the emerging trusts, or monopolies, that were gaining domination over key industries. Businessmen like John D. Rockefeller and J. P. Morgan, for example, had gradually obtained control over so much of the oil and steel industries, respectively, that they were in a position to dictate terms and

Muckrakers and the Trusts

President Roosevelt had help in understanding the implications of trusts, or monopolies, on American life. He was president at a time when crusading journalists and writers were constantly revealing excesses of corporate greed.

The Roosevelt era coincided with the era of "muckraking" journalism, a term Roosevelt coined to describe newspaper and magazine stories that revealed the everyday implications of uncontrolled corporate maneuvering.

Among the best-known muckrakers were **Jacob Riis, Ida Tarbell, Lincoln Steffens,** and **Upton Sinclair** (see entry on The Muckrakers). They wrote both nonfiction (for instance, Tarbell's 1904 book *The History of the Standard Oil Company*) and fiction (Upton Sinclair's 1906 novel *The Jungle,* about the unsanitary conditions in Chicago's stockyards) to bring home to Americans the abuses of the industrial age.

Several popular magazines, especially *Collier's* and *McClure's,* specialized in reports on abuse of power by giant companies—and at the same time made it easier for Roosevelt to use government power to address the abuses. The continuing popular appeal of these magazines was evidence of growing public discontent with the evolution of the powerful business monopolies. And continuing revelations about corporate greed made business tycoons—the Industrial Revolution's so-called robber barons—into highly unpopular symbols of the abuse of power by giant corporations.

The muckraking movement was closely aligned with the Progressive Party headed by Roosevelt in the election of 1912.

prices to their customers. Smaller firms could not compete and often ended up selling out to the trusts or simply being driven out of business. By driving competitors out of business, the trusts had consolidated not only economic power but political power as well.

The tendency of capitalists (people who own large businesses) to create anticompetitive monopolies had long been recognized; the Scottish economist **Adam Smith** (1723–1790; see entry) wrote about it in the mid-1700s. But until the time of Theodore Roosevelt, no American president had been willing to take on the giants of business, partly because politicians relied on the financial support of big business to remain in office. And most politicians in the latter half of the 1800s thought that government had no role in business and economic affairs. But in his first address to Congress, in December 1901, Roosevelt put forward a different viewpoint: "There is," he said, "a widespread conviction among the American people that the great corporations known as trusts are ... hurtful to the general welfare. It is based upon sincere conviction that combination and concentration [of business interests] should be, not prohibited, but supervised and within reasonable limits controlled."

In 1902 Roosevelt proposed—and Congress created—a Bureau of Corporations, designed to regulate the previously unregulated corporations.

Roosevelt initiated a more significant move on February 18, 1902, by filing a lawsuit against the Northern Securities Company, accusing it of violating the Sherman Antitrust Act of 1890. His choice of targets was significant: the Northern Securities Company had been organized by the foremost financier of the day, J. P. Morgan. Northern Securities was a company designed to control two railroads, the Northern Pacific and the Great Northern, which formerly had competed with one another to carry passengers and freight east-to-west across the northern tier of states. The objective of the Northern Securities Company was to organize the two railroads so that they would cooperate instead of compete. To the owner and developer of the Great Northern, **James J. Hill** (1838–1916; see entry), it was simply a question of improving efficiency.

The case worked its way through federal courts and two years after it was initially filed, the U.S. Supreme Court ruled in favor of the government. The Northern Securities Company was ordered broken up into its original companies.

Eventually, Roosevelt's government would file a total of forty-three such lawsuits, including one of the most famous that resulted in the breakup of John D. Rockefeller's Standard Oil Company in 1911, after Roosevelt had left office.

In addition to filing suits against trusts, Roosevelt was vigorous in pushing unprecedented legislation to regulate the activities of businesspeople. During his years in office, magazine stories and books published by the Muckrakers (see box on page 156) exposed corporate abuses and generated a strong public sentiment in favor of gaining control over private businesses or eliminating competition and driving independent businesspeople into financial ruin.

Was Teddy Roosevelt antibusiness?

Roosevelt's suits and legislation enraged many businessmen, who continued to feel that the government had no right to regulate business—an attitude that has persevered into the twenty-first century. To some, he was considered antibusiness.

Roosevelt saw things differently. He believed that in order to prosper, industrial-era businesses had to grow. But he realized that such growth gave corporations unprecedented social and economic power, and that government needed to step in to act as a counterbalance to that power. The economic influence exerted by huge corporations, he believed, could soon dwarf the political power of the government, resulting in a society dominated by the wealthy. It is a struggle that continues to play out in the twenty-first century.

For his part, Roosevelt had promised in 1904 that he would not run for another term in 1908. But during the term of William Howard Taft (1857–1930), the Republican who succeeded Roosevelt, the ex-president grew restless and dissatisfied with what he thought was Taft's leaning in the direction of the interests of corporate owners at the expense of ordinary voters.

In 1910 Roosevelt launched a campaign for what he called the "new nationalism," an era in which the national government would take precedence over local governments and serve an active role in regulating business for the common good. Roosevelt challenged Taft for the 1912 Republican nomination, and although he easily won in party primary elections (elections held to choose a political party's candidate for office), Roosevelt ultimately lost the nomination to Taft, who exerted his control over officials inside the Republican Party.

Not one to give up without a strenuous fight, Roosevelt switched parties and ran for president as the head of the Progressive Party (sometimes called the Bull Moose Party). Roosevelt called for a federal tax on incomes and inheritances, increased regulation of corporations, and legislation to create social justice for working people. In the election, he and Taft divided the vote of the Republicans, allowing a Democrat, Woodrow Wilson (1856–1924), to be elected president.

By then, the era of reform was largely over. Some of the muckrakers of the previous decade actively supported

Wilson, even though it was Roosevelt who started the push to regulate industrial enterprises and clean up the corruption and bribery that had allowed businesses at all levels, from local to national, to influence government.

After losing the election of 1912, Roosevelt continued to take an active role in the public arena. After World War I (1914–18) broke out in Europe in 1914, he campaigned for the United States to enter the war on the side of Britain and France. He criticized President Wilson for being too slow in mobilizing the U.S. Army once the United States did enter the war in 1917. After the war, he questioned the wisdom of the United States's joining the League of Nations, a predecessor to the United Nations that Woodrow Wilson hoped would avoid future wars.

Roosevelt was among the most influential of all presidents in shaping the future. It was he who realized the need for a new balance of power between the huge corporations born of the Industrial Revolution, and ordinary citizens as represented by the government. He addressed the balance of property rights and human rights. He saw the dangers in having a society marked by a huge imbalance of wealth, in which a handful of business owners were worth billions of dollars while millions of working people were on the verge of starvation.

Roosevelt was also responsible for the federal government taking an active role in protecting environmental treasures in the American West from unregulated economic exploitation by creating national monuments and parks.

Theodore Roosevelt died at his estate in Oyster Bay, Long Island, on January 6, 1919.

For More Information

Books

Auchincloss, Louis. *Theodore Roosevelt.* New York: Times Books/Henry Holt, 2001.

Dalton, Kathleen. *Theodore Roosevelt: A Strenuous Life.* New York: Alfred A. Knopf, 2002.

Morris, Edmund. *Theodore Rex.* New York: Random House, 2001.

Roosevelt, Theodore. *Theodore Roosevelt's Letters to His Children.* New York: Scribner's, 1919.

Schuman, Michael A. *Theodore Roosevelt.* Springfield, NJ: Enslow Publishers, 1997.

Periodicals

McCollum, Sean. "Teddy—the Bear in the Bully Pulpit: Theodore Roosevelt Could Be Brash and Outrageous, but He Shaped the Modern Presidency." *Scholastic Update,* November 3, 1997, p. 15.

Morris, Edmund. "Theodore Roosevelt, President." *American Heritage,* June–July 1981, p. 4.

Web Sites

Theodore Roosevelt Association. http://www.theodoreroosevelt.org/ (accessed on February 15, 2003).

"Theodore Roosevelt, His Life and Times on Film." *Library of Congress.* http://memory.loc.gov/ammem/trfhtml/trfhome.html (accessed on February 15, 2003).

"Theodore Roosevelt: Icon of the American Century." *Smithsonian Institution National Portrait Gallery.* http://www.npg.si.edu/exh/roosevelt/ (accessed on February 15, 2003).

Adam Smith

Born June 5, 1723
Kirkcaldy, Scotland

Died July 17, 1790
Edinburgh, Scotland

Scottish economist, philosopher

"It is not from the benevolence of the butcher, the brewer, or the baker, that we expect our dinner, but from their regard to their own interest. We address ourselves, not to their humanity but to their self-love, and never talk to them of our necessities but of their advantages."

Reproduced by permission of the Library of Congress.

Adam Smith is often regarded as providing the theoretical justification for the Industrial Revolution, a period of fast-paced economic change that began in Great Britain in the middle of the eighteenth century. His masterpiece, *An Inquiry Into the Nature and Causes of the Wealth of Nations* (familiarly known by its abbreviated title *The Wealth of Nations,* 1776), was published just as the Industrial Revolution was gaining momentum in England. In it Smith argued that economic competition, rather than government regulation, was the best way to assure the greatest good for the greatest number of people. Despite this belief, Smith recognized an important role for government in making sure that business owners did not conspire to limit competition for their selfish interests.

What is the best way to assure maximum happiness for the greatest number of people? Aside from the realm of personal relationships between individuals, this question often involves the subject of economics, the systematic study of how people create wealth and how societies distribute it.

Smith was one of the first philosophers to consider this subject comprehensively, and his theories still have many advocates in the twenty-first century. He is sometimes considered the intellectual godfather of capitalism, the system that leaves ownership of factories and other types of property in private hands.

Smith's writings played an important part in gaining widespread acceptance of the capitalist economic system that came into being in Britain and the United States, namely regulated free-enterprise. Much of the economic and political history of both the United States and Britain since the late eighteenth century could be described as an ongoing series of experiments to achieve the ideal balance between individual economic freedom and social restraints (or government controls) that Smith thought offered the best chance for the greatest happiness for the greatest number of people.

Childhood and early years

Adam Smith was born in Kirkcaldy, Scotland in 1723. His father was a government official at Kirkcaldy, and he died two months before Adam was born. Adam grew up as an adoring, and adored, only son. He was not especially healthy as an infant, and in later years his mother, Margaret Douglas, was criticized for spoiling her child. Adam remained devoted to his mother for his entire life.

The most dramatic incident recorded in Adam's childhood occurred when he was about three years old. He and his mother were visiting Adam's uncle in Strathenry, Scotland, and Adam was left playing outside in the courtyard. A small group of homeless people came across the child and kidnapped him. His uncle heard the footsteps and quickly gave chase, rescuing his young nephew.

As a young boy, Adam was not physically strong enough for vigorous play. Instead, he became an avid reader. He was remembered as having a warm, friendly, and generous personality, and he had many friends.

At age fourteen, Smith became a student at the small but influential University of Glasgow for three years. In 1740, at age seventeen, he traveled to England and enrolled in Balliol College of Oxford University, where he was a student for nearly seven years. Attending college in Smith's era was quite

a different experience from what it is today. Attendance at classes was voluntary and lecturers were often paid by students, much as if going to a film or play. Smith earned his bachelor of arts degree from Oxford and returned to his hometown of Kirkcaldy, where he resumed living with his mother. He earned money by giving lectures on English literature until he decided to move to Edinburgh, Scotland.

Adam Smith attended Balliol College at Oxford University, pictured, for seven years, and became one of the premier economists of his or any other era. *Reproduced by permission of the Corbis Corporation.*

In 1751, at age twenty-seven, Smith became a professor of logic at the University of Glasgow and later became a professor of moral philosophy. Eight years later, he published the first of his two principal works: *The Theory of Moral Sentiments.* The book laid out Smith's ideas on morality, which he thought were based on the idea of sympathy (that is, human beings can easily imagine being in someone else's position), and ideas of right and wrong essentially stem from the notion of sympathy for another person, he reasoned.

In 1764 Smith was offered an opportunity to travel across Europe as a tutor to two young Scottish aristocrats, sons of the duke of Buccleuch. Their itinerary included visits to Paris, Toulouse, and Geneva during a period of intense intellectual activity in Europe that eventually led up to the French Revolution in 1789. On the trip, Smith met some French physiocrats, economists who believed that agriculture was the only true source of a nation's added wealth. It was an economic idea that gained popularity in France at just the time that the Industrial Revolution was about to take off in England, helping to explain why industrialization was initially more widely accepted in England than in France.

Smith returned to Scotland in 1766. He moved back in with his mother and a cousin, and spent the next ten years producing his major work: a book on economics titled *An Inquiry Into the Nature and Causes of the Wealth of Nations.*

The Wealth of Nations

Smith's nine-hundred-page book presents both an analysis of economics and a series of policy recommendations. Using historical and contemporary examples, he explains the principles of economics and, in particular, why some nations are wealthy and others are not.

In considering Adam Smith, it is essential to bear in mind that he published his book in the midst of the era of mercantilism, an economic theory that advocated government control over foreign trade. This theory had been dominant in England, France, and Holland since about 1500. In brief, it held that the best way for a country to increase its overall wealth was to increase export of manufactured goods, for example, in exchange for gold or silver, which was needed to pay for armies and the costs of government.

Ideally, according to the mercantilist system, governments would use armies to protect foreign trade in which manufactured goods were sold abroad for gold or silver. The government was chiefly in control of foreign trade, with the objective of selling more abroad than was purchased, and also of encouraging manufacturing over, say, agriculture or mining. Thus, government policy was aimed at regulating the economy to make sure manufacturing was favored, and that foreign trade resulted in a balance favorable to the home country.

When the British government applied this philosophy to its North American colonies, it eventually alienated the colonists. For example, the government in London insisted that the colonies trade exclusively with England, even if better deals could be had by the colonists in trading with such countries as France or Holland. Over the years, this insistence on uneven trade and exclusive dealing with England increasingly angered American colonists and helped bring on the American Revolution (1775–83).

The invisible hand

Smith's book was largely a rejection of mercantilism. He favored instead a theory that is sometimes shortened to "the invisible hand." Smith contended that the way to achieve the ideal economic result for everyone was to let competition run its course; if every individual is left free to pursue his or her own vision of what is best, the overall total result for everyone will turn out to be good. Smith reasoned, for example, that under a system of free trading, each individual would do what he or she did best, such as making shoes or furniture. Thus, those who were good at making shoes would thrive in the shoemaking industry, while those who were especially talented at making furniture would concentrate their expertise in that industry.

Smith urged adoption of a few basic policies by governments eager to achieve the best economic result. Foremost was free trade, the elimination of restrictions on the purchase and sale of goods between countries. Similarly, if merchants are given legal monopolies on exporting or importing certain goods, this will result in artificially inflated prices and disturb the most efficient distribution of resources. Instead, let those who can produce a product most inexpensively have an opportunity to do so and pass along this advantage to everyone in the society.

Smith explained his notion that free trade encourages individuals to seek fulfilling occupations. "As it is the power of exchanging that gives occasion to the division of labor, so the extent of this division must always be limited by the extent ... of the market," he wrote in *The Wealth of Nations.*

That is, a bigger market will result in a greater, and more efficient, division of labor.

Sometimes Smith's idea of freedom of trade is oversimplified and presented as the notion of laissez-faire (pronounced lay-zay-FAIR; a French expression meaning "free to do," suggesting that people should be free to do as they choose). In fact, Smith never advocated laissez-faire. He realized that business people are likely to get together and make secret arrangements (such as agreeing to charge the same price for items in short supply, or buying other companies in order to eliminate competition) that will benefit themselves at the public's expense.

In Smith's words: "People of the same trade seldom meet together, even for merriment and diversion, [without] the conversation [ending] in a conspiracy against the public, or in some contrivance to raise prices."

When they can, business owners will join in societies designed to promote their special interests, often at the expense of the overall interests of their societies, Smith thought. He wrote in *The Wealth of Nations*:

> The proposal of any new law or regulation of commerce which comes from this order, ought always to be listened to with great precaution, and ought never to be adopted till after having been long and carefully examined, not only with the most scrupulous, but with the most suspicious attention. It comes from an order of men, whose interest is never exactly the same with that of the public, who have generally an interest to deceive and even to oppress the public, and who accordingly have, upon many occasions, both deceived and oppressed it.

Smith saw three main functions for government: defending the nation from attack; providing a system of law to protect the rights of property, punish fraud, enforce contracts, and prevent violence; and providing public services, such as building roads, that no one in private business was likely to produce.

Smith also believed that economic competition and government regulation would work together to protect the public from the tendency by businesspeople to conspire against the public interest. At the same time, he recognized that there might be some instances in which a country's best interests were served by the government granting a merchant a special set of rights in order to encourage setting up trade with a particular country or in a particular commodity (something needed for defense purposes, for instance) that might not normally be profitable.

Smith accepted that under capitalism, wealthy businesspeople would tend to grow steadily richer. But he thought workers also would come to be better off over time.

An unfinished script

Although Smith was explicit in believing that businesspeople would tend to conspire against the public good, he did not make it clear exactly how governments should be organized to prevent this. Based on his own experience with government mercantile policies, he clearly understood how merchants would try to persuade governments to adopt policies that were in their narrow interests—and against the broader interests of the society.

Nevertheless, Smith provided many generations of economists and politicians arguments in favor of letting business grow without interference from government. The Industrial Revolution resulted in business enterprises much larger and more influential than any previously seen, and consequently social power in the hands of business owners that was much greater than the powers previously exercised by merchants or landowners. When this power was questioned, generations of businesspeople could point to the writings of Adam Smith as an argument for keeping government out of the business of business.

Near the time of his death, Smith was working on a third work, but illness made it impossible for him to complete the book. Not long before he died, he asked that his papers be burned. "What remains," he wrote in *The Theory of Moral Sentiments,* "the theory of jurisprudence, which I have long projected, I have hitherto been hindered from executing.... My very advanced age leaves me ... very little expectation of ever being able to execute this great work to my own satisfaction."

The Wealth of Nations was a critical and popular success during Smith's lifetime. Within a few years of its publication, many of Smith's recommendations became law, even as England advanced quickly as the leader in the Industrial Revolution.

In 1790, at the age of sixty-seven, Adam Smith died in Edinburgh, Scotland.

For More Information

Books

Macfarlane, Alan. *The Riddle of the Modern World: Of Liberty, Wealth and Equality.* New York: St. Martin's Press, 2000.

Ross, Ian Simpson. *The Life of Adam Smith.* Oxford, England: Clarendon Press, 1995.

Rothschild, Emma. *Economic Sentiments: Adam Smith, Condorcet, and the Enlightenment.* Cambridge, MA: Harvard University Press, 2001.

Smith, Adam. *The Essential Adam Smith.* New York: W. W. Norton, 1987.

Smith, Adam. *An Inquiry Into the Nature and Causes of the Wealth of Nations.* New York: Modern Library, 1994.

Smith, Adam. *The Theory of Moral Sentiments.* Oxford, England: Clarendon Press, 1976.

Periodicals

Gordon, John Steele. "Land of the Free Trade." *American Heritage,* July–August 1993, p. 50.

Kaufman, Henry. "If Adam Smith Were Alive Today: Capitalism Is the Only Way to Go." *Vital Speeches,* October 15, 2001, p. 12.

Web Sites

"Adam Smith 1723–1790." *History of Economic Thought.* http://cepa.newschool.edu/het/profiles/smith.htm (accessed on February 15, 2003).

"Adam Smith (1723–90)." *The Library of Economics and Liberty.* http://www. econlib.org/library/Enc/bios/Smith.html (accessed on February 15, 2003).

Yardeni, Edward and David A. Moss. "The Triumph of Adam Smith." *The Library of Economics and Liberty.* http://www.adamsmith.org.uk/smith/triumph-of-smith.pdf (accessed on February 15, 2003).

George Stephenson

Born June 9, 1781
Wylam, England

Died August 12, 1848
Chesterfield, England

British engineer, inventor

"I put up with every rebuff, and went on with my plans, determined not to be put down."

Reproduced by permission of the Library of Congress.

George Stephenson was a largely self-taught engineer who developed the steam blast locomotive, or railroad engine. Stephenson became the leading manufacturer of railroads and locomotives in England at the height of the Industrial Revolution, a period of fast-paced economic change that began in Great Britain in the middle of the eighteenth century. The Industrial Revolution resulted in many changes in societies where it took place, especially England. One of those changes was to open new prospects for success and wealth to people born into modest circumstances.

Such was the case with Stephenson, whose father worked in a coal mine and who himself spent his childhood working to earn money for his family. By the time Stephenson died, however, at age sixty-seven, he had achieved wealth and fame as the foremost manufacturer of locomotives and entire railroads in England. He did this not by accident of birth, that is, by inheriting wealth and position, but by dint of his abilities as an engineer.

Childhood and youth

George Stephenson was born on June 9, 1781, in the small town of Wylam, near Newcastle-on-Tyne, in England. His family's cottage was located next to the Wylam wagonway, a set of wooden tracks that carried wagons loaded with coal from the nearby mine to the Tyne River. The wooden wagonway came before the iron (and later, steel) railroad tracks that were needed to bear the weight of locomotives.

Coal miners in the late eighteenth century were paid barely enough to live on, and their children usually had to take small jobs to help the family pay its bills. George's first job as a boy of eight was herding cows and driving horses for the coal mine's "gin," a machine used to move weights. When he was fourteen, George got a job in the mine, working alongside his father as an assistant fireman. Within a year, George had become a fireman, and two years later was promoted to the job of "plug man," the person responsible for keeping mine ore moving through the chutes that moved coal from one level to another.

After working in the coal mine during the day, George attended school at night to learn how to read and write. A man of enormous energy, he also occasionally mended boots for extra money.

In 1802 Stephenson married Frances Henderson, who worked as a servant on a nearby farm. The following year they had a son, whom they named Robert, after his grandfather. Stephenson and his son Robert had an extraordinary lifetime partnership, begun perhaps when Frances died of tuberculosis in 1806 while Robert was still a toddler. Tuberculosis, a lung disease caused by a bacterium, is easily communicable and was commonplace in the era before antibiotics.

A fascination with locomotives

Even as a boy, Stephenson had been fascinated by the machines that ran along the wagonway next to his house. His work around steam engines in the coal mines increased his fascination with all things mechanical.

Stephenson was also determined to improve his education. When his son came of age, his father sent him to school in Newcastle, England. At night, father and son worked together on the boy's homework, and in this way Stephenson learned mathematics, which he would put to use a few years later as he began designing locomotives.

Years later, according to author Frederick S. Williams in *Our Iron Roads,* Stephenson recalled in a speech at the opening of the Newcastle and Darlington Railway in 1844:

> When he [Robert] was a little boy, I saw how deficient I was in education, and made up my mind that he should not labor under the same defect, but that I would put him to a good school, and give him a liberal training. I was, however, a poor man; and how do you think I managed. I betook myself to mending my neighbors' clocks and watches at night, after my daily labor was done; and thus I procured the means of educating my son. He became my assistant and my companion.... At night we worked together at our engineering.

At age twenty-seven, Stephenson got a job as engineman at the Killingworth coal mine. One of the dangers that plagued coal miners at the time was methane, an explosive gas that accumulated in mines. Occasionally, miners' lamps would touch off a deadly explosion. In 1815 Stephenson developed a new lamp that would not spark an explosion. The invention added greatly to Stephenson's reputation as a budding engineer. (At the same time, one of England's most important scientists, Humphrey Davy [1778–1829], developed a similar lamp, leading to a long argument between the two men over who came up with the idea first. Apparently, it was a case of both men simultaneously having a similar idea.)

Stephenson's big break

By 1812, Stephenson's sophistication with engines led to his becoming the Killingworth mine's enginewright, a job that involved repairing and manufacturing engines. The following year, he learned of efforts to develop a steam-powered locomotive at the nearby Wylam coal mine. He suggested to the manager of the Killingworth mine that he could develop a locomotive himself—and the manager agreed to let him try.

In 1814, Stephenson's locomotive, called the *Blutcher,* was running, able to pull 30 tons (60,000 pounds) of coal ore uphill at 4 miles an hour. Stephenson's locomotive was not the only one developed at the time, however. But it did have

Other Locomotive Pioneers

George Stephenson was not the only engineer engaged in building locomotives in the early nineteenth century. Other coal mines had the same requirements as Stephenson's and funded designs of similar engines.

Richard Trevithick (1771–1833) was among the most famous, but least successful, pioneers in developing locomotives. Like George Stephenson, Trevithick was a mine engineer when he developed a miniature locomotive in 1796. In 1801 Trevithick demonstrated a larger working version, called *Puffing Devil,* by taking seven friends for a ride on Christmas Eve. But the locomotive only worked on short trips since it could not maintain steam pressure for long. **James Watt** (1736–1819; see entry), developer of the steam engine, saw *Puffing Devil* and thought that it posed a danger of exploding.

A series of other locomotives designed by Trevithick also failed; most proved too heavy for the cast iron rails they ran over. Trevithick eventually moved to Peru to work as an engineer in a silver mine. There, his engines were successful, and he earned enough money to buy his own silver mine. But fighting during Peru's war for independence from Spain forced Trevithick to abandon his property and flee to Colombia in 1826. There, he met Robert Stephenson, who was building a railway. Stephenson sympathized with his

some unique features, notably the fact that the steam engine applied its power directly to the locomotive's flanged wheels. (On railroad cars and engines, a flange is a rim around the edge of the wheel that prevents the wheel from slipping sideways off the rail.)

Over the next five years, Stephenson built sixteen locomotives at Killingworth mine, mostly for use in the mine, but a few for use on a wagonway owned by the duke of Portland. Stephenson's work so impressed his employer that in 1819 the mine asked him to build a railroad 8 miles long, between the town of Hetton and the River Wear. For this project, Stephenson proposed a combination of locomotives and stationary engines. Locomotives hauled the loaded cars over the first, relatively level, section of track. Then they were pulled uphill by a steam engine at the top of the hill, using cables. The cars then coasted downhill, where another fixed fellow English railroad pioneer and gave Trevithick enough money to get back to London. In 1828 George Stephenson credited Trevithick with important contributions in the evolution of the locomotive, but despite Stephenson's endorsement, Parliament (the British government) declined funding to pay Trevithick a pension (money paid in retirement). He died in extreme poverty in 1833.

William Hedley (1779–1843) was managing the Wylam coal mine in 1808 when the owner asked him to produce a steam locomotive. Hedley first introduced a system of smooth iron rails, convinced that the weight of the locomotive would produce enough traction. In 1814 Hedley produced a working locomotive that ran on eight wheels, instead of four, thereby distributing the weight so that the rails could support it.

In 1814 Hedley, aided by two craftsmen at the mine, Jonathan Foster and Timothy Hackworth, produced a working locomotive at almost the same time as George Stephenson. The design differed, principally in the way the steam engine delivered power to the wheels, but the Hedley model worked. Two engines he produced—including the *Puffing Billy* and the *Wylam Dilly*—were still functioning sixty years later.

engine, located at the top of the next hill, pulled them to the top. It was the first railway powered entirely by machines, with no animals used.

Working on this project, Stephenson realized that it would be a huge advantage if the railway could be built to be as level as possible. This project launched Stephenson on the second part of his career: that of a builder of railways.

In 1821 the British Parliament authorized the construction of a horse railway to connect coal mines in West Durham and Darlington, England, to the River Tees. Stephenson arranged a meeting with the owner of the company building the railway and told him that his *Blutcher* locomotive, which runs on iron tracks, could replace fifty horses.

Stephenson's argument was persuasive, and the Stockton and Darlington Railway gave the job to him. With his son

George and Robert Stephenson's prize-winning locomotive, *Rocket* (pictured), established them as the leading builders of locomotives in England. *Reproduced by permission of the Library of Congress.*

as his partner, Stephenson formed Robert Stephenson and Company, headquartered in Newcastle, England, to build the railway and the locomotives that would be used on it. It was the world's first company formed to produce locomotives.

On September 27, 1825, Stephenson operated his new engine, named *Locomotion,* along the nine-mile railroad in just less than two hours.

Success builds on success

The Stockton and Darlington Railway was the first of many successes enjoyed by George and Robert Stephenson. As railways started to replace canals for transporting heavy loads, their firm was hired to build other railways, including their biggest triumph, the Liverpool and Manchester Railway, designed to link England's greatest manufacturing center, Manchester, with the port city of Liverpool.

In 1828 the directors of the railway held a contest to see whose locomotives would be used on the line. In addition to the contract for building the locomotive, the winner was to receive a substantial cash prize. Ten locomotives were entered into the contest in October 1829. Of the ten, only five arrived on the day of the competition, and two of these were ruled out as being too heavy for the rails. Competitors' locomotives were required to run up and down the track at Rainhill, hauling a load three times the locomotive's own weight, at a speed of 10 miles an hour, for a distance equivalent to a round trip between Liverpool and Manchester.

The Stephensons's entry, *Rocket,* won the competition, thereby cementing their reputation as England's leading builders of locomotives.

Two years later, the Liverpool and Manchester Railway opened with ceremonies that included the British prime minister, the duke of Wellington, and other prominent people, plus a procession of locomotives. The ceremony was marred when one government minister was hit by a locomotive and killed, but the Liverpool and Manchester Railway itself was a great success and led to much more business for Robert Stephenson and Company.

In 1838 Stephenson's business success enabled him to buy a mansion, named Tapton House, a far cry from the modest cottage next to the Wylam wagonway where he had been born. He invested in coal mines and ironworks and experimented with agriculture, including a scheme to increase the productivity of chickens by shutting them in dark henhouses after they ate. Stephenson's dual success at engineering and business was an early example of how the Industrial Revolution changed the prospects for bright young people of modest beginnings.

Stephenson died at Tapton House on August 12, 1848.

For More Information

Books

Nock, O. S. *Father of Railways: The Story of George Stephenson.* Edinburgh, Scotland: T. Nelson, 1958.

Rolt, L. T. C. *The Railway Revolution: George and Robert Stephenson.* New York: St. Martin's Press, 1962.

Smiles, Samuel. *The Life of George Stephenson, Railway Engineer.* Ann Arbor, MI: Plutarch Press, 1971.

Periodicals

Lynn, Jack. "Secrets of Seven Self-made Millionaires." *Washingtonian,* February 1981, p. 100.

Web Sites

"George Stephenson, a Biography of the English Inventor and Railroad Pioneer." *Britain Express.* http://www.britainexpress.com/History/bio/stephenson.htm (accessed on February 17, 2003).

"Some Historical Background to the Liverpool and Manchester Railway." *Resco Railways Ltd.* http://www.resco.co.uk/iron.html (accessed on February 17, 2003).

Williams, Frederick S. "Our Iron Roads." *Resco Railways Ltd.* http://www.resco.co.uk/stevensons.html (accessed on February 17, 2003).

James Watt

Born January 19, 1736
Greenock, Scotland

Died August 25, 1819
Heathfield, England

Scottish engineer, inventor

"The problem of which Watt solved a part is not the problem of inventing a machine, but the problem of using and storing the forces of nature which now go to waste."

—Andrew Carnegie on James Watt.

James Watt is often credited with inventing the steam engine, but this distinction belongs to others. Instead, he adapted the invention of others to make the steam engine a practicable means of providing power to operate a wide range of machines. Such machines were the hallmark of the Industrial Revolution, a period of fast-paced economic change that began in Great Britain in the middle of the eighteenth century. In this sense, James Watt could be described as the father of the Industrial Revolution.

Watt's steam engine was the one innovation that did the most to change the way human beings lived and worked after about 1750. Watt's contribution was to increase the efficiency of the steam engine, so that it burned less coal for the same amount of energy produced. Earlier models used about four times as much coal as Watt's engine. Throughout his life Watt experimented and improved on his engine, refining systems that provide the basis for many industrial engines used today.

Reproduced by permission of the Library of Congress.

Universal Public Education

Following the teaching of Scottish Protestant leader John Knox, a law passed in 1696 required families to send children to school, rather than employing them in home-based cottage industries like spinning and weaving. Scotland had one of the first laws making education of children compulsory.

Birth and childhood

On January 19, 1736, Agnes Muirhead Watt gave birth to her fourth child, a baby boy. She and her husband named him James, after his father. The Watt family lived in the small seaport town of Greenock, Scotland. James Watt senior made a living however he could, working variously as a merchant, a carpenter, and a government administrator. Young James frequently assisted his father as a carpenter and from an early age enjoyed carpenter's tools more than books.

James was somewhat sickly and could not attend school as a young boy. Since three of the Watt babies had died in infancy, his mother was not inclined to send her boy out of the house when he was not well. But James learned well at home. Agnes read to her son and taught him to read. The home in which James grew up was well equipped with tools from his father's carpentry business, and as a young boy James received his own set of small tools from his father. James made good use of these tools. First he watched the skilled workmen in his father's shop, then he retreated to his room to practice taking apart and putting together navigation instruments or making miniature models of machines. The Watt family fit the pattern of craftspeople working at home that prevailed in Europe right up to the time of the Industrial Revolution.

When James was eighteen, his mother died and his father's fortunes declined. It was the beginning of a difficult period for Watt, and one that had a profound impact on his future career. Watt would become an apprentice (an assistant learning a trade) instead of following his father's failing business or going to the university.

Apprenticeship and early career

In 1754, at age eighteen, Watt left home for London, England, determined to apprentice himself to a master scientific instrument maker. It was a time when measuring things, such as distances, temperatures, and weight, was the chief occupation of most scientists.

Once in London, Watt obtained a job in the workshop of John Morgan, who made mathematical instruments. For the next year, Watt worked day and night. At the end of twelve months, he returned to his family home in Scotland, ready to look for a job as an instrument maker.

Watt's apprenticeship was a critical turning point. Had his father been able to afford it, chances are Watt would have attended the University of Glasgow, perhaps to become a mathematician like his grandfather. Instead, he went in the direction of working with his hands—as well as his head—and, of necessity, his mind turned toward the practical rather than the theoretical.

James Watt Timeline

1736: Born in Greenock, Scotland, on January 19.

1754: Goes to London as an apprentice to a mathematical instrument maker.

1759: Opens shop in Glasgow, Scotland, to make instruments and toys.

1764: Marries Margaret Miller. Asked to repair a model of the Newcomen steam engine.

1775: Enters into partnership with Matthew Boulton.

1781: Invents rotary motion device for his steam engine.

1819: Dies on August 25, at age eighty-four.

Shortly after his return from London, Watt was asked to repair an astronomical instrument given to the University of Glasgow. His repair was done so well that in 1757 the university offered him a job making and repairing scientific instruments for the mathematics department. The job provided a place to live and a workshop.

Watt's new position put him in the midst of other young men who had an intense interest in developments in science. Through his association with students and young faculty members, Watt acquired an extensive education in science, including physics, chemistry, and math.

Watt's business was thriving, especially from jobs he was given from outside the university. In October 1759 Watt entered into a partnership with an architect named John Craig, and opened his own shop in Glasgow. The business grew and soon there was a need for a larger shop, where sixteen men were kept busy. The partnership ended with Craig's death in 1765.

Joseph Black

Joseph Black was one of the young men at the University of Glasgow who associated with James Watt. Born in 1728, Black studied medicine, but his greatest interest was in chemistry, and he become preeminent in that field. Among the many subjects Black studied, his observations on heat and steam were central to James Watt's work. At first, though, the relationship was the other way around: Watt helped Black with his work by making scientific instruments—critical to enable scientists like Black to take precise measurements in their laboratory experiments.

Black's main inquiries concerned the nature of heat and what happens when a hot object comes into contact with a cold one. At the time, scientists believed that objects had a mysterious quality called "caloric"—in essence, that objects contained "heat" that was transferred to colder bodies upon contact until the caloric in both bodies was equally distributed. Black conducted a range of experiments, measuring how heat was transferred between objects, especially water. Black's observations, later tested and confirmed by Watt, were a key ingredient in generating power by heating water until it turns to steam, and then cooling it again.

Repairing a model steam engine

In the winter of 1763–64, Watt was asked to do another task in his university workshop: to repair a model of the steam engine that had been developed by Englishman Thomas Newcomen (1663–1729). Newcomen's early steam engine was similar to one made even earlier, in 1678, by another British inventor, Thomas Savery. By 1763, Newcomen's engine was widely used in Britain and its North American colonies to pump water out of coal mine shafts.

But Newcomen's engine was inefficient. It required enormous quantities of coal and three men to keep it running, and it operated slowly at only about ten strokes per minute. (A stroke is the movement of a piston from the top of the cylinder to the bottom, and back to the top.) Another disadvantage was that Newcomen's engine produced only a reciprocating movement, meaning that it moved strictly up and down. Much later, in 1781, Watt designed an engine that converted this reciprocating motion to one of rotation, which was much more useful in driving the machinery in factories and mills, as opposed to pumping water.

As he was repairing the model of a Newcomen engine, Watt began experimenting with some improvements. It was characteristic of Watt's work that he combined his knowledge of engineering—materials and mechanics—and his knowledge of physics—the qualities of steam and atmospheric pressure—to design a better engine.

In 1765 Watt made a model of his new steam engine. Four years later, in 1769, he patented it, but waited seven more years to work seriously on the idea that would bring him fame. And it took three more years until Watt's steam engine was put into practical use.

Business partnership and fortune

In 1769 Watt set about constructing a steam engine on the new principles he discovered while working on the Newcomen model. To help finance the project, he entered into a partnership with a doctor and businessman named John Roebuck (1718–1794). The business arrangement was not really a success, but Watt did manage to get a model of his new design up and working.

Five years later, in 1775, Watt once again formed a partnership, this time with industrialist Matthew Boulton (1728–1809). Boulton had a buckle-making factory near Birmingham, England, that employed about six hundred people. He was interested in discovering ways that science could help improve his business.

Under their arrangement, Boulton received two-thirds of the rights to Watt's patent for a steam engine; Watt received a salary, plus the full expenses of manufacturing the engines. It was this partnership that would at last work.

It took a year for the new firm of Boulton and Watt to produce their first steam engine. Finally, on March 8, 1776, a machine they were building to help pump water from a coal mine was demonstrated. A reporter from the *Birmingham Gazette* attended the demonstration and wrote: "Curiosity was excited to see the first movement of so singular and powerful a machine; and whose expectations were fully gratified by the excellence of its performance."

One great improvement of Watt's steam engine over the older Newcomen model was that it used only about one-fourth as much coal to achieve the same power. This proved to be an important factor in the business success of Boulton and Watt.

In 1786 Watt's company began building steam engines to operate cotton mills. It was an important develop-

Did You Know?

James Watt's name is found in practically every room in the United States—printed on lightbulbs. The "watt" is a measure of power, and it was named in honor of James Watt. Strangely, James Watt had nothing to do with electricity or lighting. His expertise was in the ability of steam to transmit power.

ment. Cotton clothes were in wide demand, colonists in America were growing plenty of cotton to supply the industry, and Watt's steam engine made the mills much more productive. The steam engine revolutionized the textile industry.

In 1800, at age sixty-four, Watt retired to a happy life in the country. But his curiosity and love of making things did not end with retirement. He moved back to Birmingham from the country and joined the Lunar Society, a group of intellectuals organized by Matthew Boulton. Watt set up a workshop in his attic; it can still be seen in a museum in London.

In his old age, Watt received many honors and much recognition. In 1784 he had been elected a member of the Royal Society in Edinburgh, Scotland. In 1785 he was elected to the Royal Society of London. In 1806 he received an honorary degree from the University of Glasgow, where he had worked as an instrument maker many years earlier. He received honors from Holland and France as well.

At the end of his life, Watt saw the Industrial Revolution fully launched. He wrote:

> I have spent a long time in improving the arts and manufactures of the nation. My inventions at present, or lately, giving employment to the best part of a million people, and having added many millions to the natural riches, and therefore I have a natural right to rest in my extreme old age.

On August 25, 1819, Watt died at his home at age eighty-four. A few years later, a statue of Watt was placed in Westminster Abbey, in London, with this inscription:

> JAMES WATT
> Who, directing the forces of an original genius,
> Early exercised in philosophic research
> to the improvement of
> THE STEAM ENGINE,
> enlarged the resources of his country

increased the power of men,
and rose to an eminent place among the most
illustrious followers of science and the real
benefactors of the world.

For More Information

Books

Crowther, J. G. *Scientists of the Industrial Revolution: Joseph Black, James Watt, Joseph Priestley, Henry Cavendish.* Philadelphia, PA: Dufour Editions, 1963.

Hart, Ivor Blashka. *James Watt and the History of Steam Power.* New York: H. Schuman, 1949.

Quackenbush, Robert M. *Watt Got You Started, Mr. Fulton?: A Story of James Watt and Robert Fulton.* Englewood Cliffs, NJ: Prentice-Hall, 1982.

Webb, Robert N. *James Watt, Inventor of a Steam Engine.* New York: F. Watts, 1970.

Periodicals

Pain, Stephanie. "The Flute-Maker's Fiddle." *New Scientist,* March 9, 2002, p. 48.

Wheeler, Mark. "Declaration of Independence: When Thomas Jefferson Wanted to Preserve His Papers, He Couldn't Wait for Xerox. So He Found a Way to Make Copies on His Own." *Inc.,* September 17, 1996, p. 72.

Web Sites

Carnegie, Andrew. "James Watt." *Steam Engine Library.* http://www.history.rochester.edu/steam/carnegie/ (accessed on February 18, 2003).

"James Watt: Fascinating Facts about James Watt and His Improvements to the Steam Engine in 1769." *The Great Idea Finder.* http://www.ideafinder.com/history/inventors/watt.htm (accessed on February 18, 2003).

Marshall, Thomas H. "James Watt." *Steam Engine Library.* http://www.history.rochester.edu/steam/marshall/ (accessed on February 18, 2003).

George Westinghouse

Born October 6, 1846
Central Bridge, New York

Died March 12, 1914
New York, New York

Nikola Tesla

Born July 10, 1856
Smiljan, Croatia

Died January 7, 1943
New York, New York

American inventors

"George Westinghouse was a man with tremendous potential energy of which only part had taken kinetic (moving) form.... When others would give up in despair, he triumphed."

—Nikola Tesla on George Westinghouse.

George Westinghouse. *Reproduced by permission of AP/Wide World Photos.*

George Westinghouse and Nikola Tesla were highly intelligent inventors who together were responsible for a major turning point in the Industrial Revolution, a period of fast-paced economic change that began in Great Britain in the middle of the eighteenth century. Tesla developed a generator, a machine that converts mechanical energy into electrical energy, which made it possible to power motors using alternating current (AC). Westinghouse, having already made a fortune by inventing the air brake, bought the patent Tesla had obtained for his AC motor and then hired him to work at his Pennsylvania manufacturing plant.

Westinghouse stood out as both a great inventor and a shrewd businessman. In an era when railroads were spreading rapidly and a way of stopping long freight trains was critical, there was a great demand for his air brakes. He later made an even more profound contribution by making possible the widespread use of electricity used for lighting, motors, and home appliances.

Tesla was undoubtedly one of the greatest inventive geniuses of the Industrial Revolution. Besides championing

AC and developing the generator, he invented an early speedometer and radio-controlled devices. And it can be argued that he invented the radio. Before his death in 1943, Tesla had acquired more than one hundred patents. His famous Tesla coil and other inventions have since become integral to modern technology.

The genius of Westinghouse

George Westinghouse was the son of a modestly successful manufacturer of agricultural machinery. As a boy, George greatly preferred working in his father's shop to going to school. At age ten, his family moved to Schenectady, New York, where George established his own workshop in the attic of the family home.

The story is told that his father agreed to pay George fifty cents a day to cut pipe into specified lengths. Young George agreed, and within just a few hours he invented a machine to do the cutting. It was only the first of many useful George Westinghouse inventions. At age fifteen, he developed a form of rotary steam-engine (one that made a circular motion, rather than the established up-and-down motion of pistons).

During the U.S. Civil War (1861–65), Westinghouse served first in the Union (that of the Northern states) cavalry, then in the U.S. Navy as an assistant engineer. Later, he enrolled in Union College, but dropped out after a year to work on his inventions. In 1865 he patented a device to get derailed railroad cars back onto the rails.

Westinghouse the inventor

Westinghouse was twenty-three years old when he developed the device that would earn him his first fortune: railroad air brakes, which he patented in 1869. Railroads were rapidly expanding as a means of hauling heavy loads of ore, coal, and manufactured goods over long distances, but they had one big disadvantage: to stop a train, brakes had to be applied by hand on each car, plus on the locomotive. This drawback limited the speed and length of trains, and also contributed to frequent accidents. Westinghouse's invention enabled the locomotive engineer to apply powerful brakes

The Life of George Westinghouse at a Glance

1846: Born in Central Bridge, New York.

1865: Receives his first patent—for rotary steam engine.

1869: Patents the air brake; forms Westinghouse Air Brake Company.

1881: Forms Westinghouse Machine Company.

1882: Organizes Union Switch and Signal Company.

1886: Forms Westinghouse Electric Company, later called Westinghouse Electric and Manufacturing Company.

1890: Begins manufacturing electric motors for railroads.

1893: Westinghouse Electric company lights the Columbian Exposition (Fair) in Chicago.

1895: Uses Niagara Falls to generate electricity.

1898–1903: Organizes subsidiaries in Russia, Britain, France, Germany, and Canada.

1905: Converts New York City subways and elevated trains to electric power.

1907: Financial panic (stock market crash and run on banks) causes Westinghouse to lose control of his companies.

1914: Dies in New York.

1918: Receives his last patent, four years after his death.

along the length of the train, which made trains safer and more manageable, and it also allowed them to run at higher speeds.

Armed with his patent, Westinghouse took the next step and formed the Westinghouse Air Brake Company. His invention made the company a fortune, but it was typical of Westinghouse that he did not stop there; this was just the first of many companies he formed to manufacture and sell inventions, either his own or those of others.

Westinghouse had been able to see the "big picture" of how things work. He realized that his air brake was not just a brake, but a system for controlling trains. This led to his next invention: a railroad signaling system that used electricity to tell locomotive engineers when to stop and when to go. As railroads were just developing, many stretches of the railroad had just one pair of rails, so trains had to stop at designated places to allow for the passage of oncoming trains. Like the air brake, Westinghouse's signaling system was an almost immediate success. It also introduced him to the potential of electricity.

Westinghouse the businessman

Westinghouse was not just a great inventor. The history of the Industrial Revolution is filled with stories of inventors who were never able to make money from their ideas, demonstrating that cleverness in design or engineering is only half the formula for success. The other half is establishing and running successful business enterprises, which Westinghouse did.

The key to success for Westinghouse was to form a new company right after he patented a new invention, to make sure that he would benefit from the idea. He applied the principle not only in the United States, but overseas as well, establishing companies in the major European countries to manufacture and sell his system of automatic air brakes for railroads.

Westinghouse's inventive genius did not prevent him from recognizing the importance of other inventors' contributions. In 1888 Westinghouse acquired the rights held by another inventor, Nikola Tesla, to develop and use alternating current (AC) instead of the direct current (DC), which was favored by the already famous Thomas Edison (1847–1931). Westinghouse invited Tesla to come work for him and provided him with sophisticated research facilities.

Nikola Tesla and the age of electricity

Nikola Tesla could easily fill the role of a classic mad scientist. He imagined things that other men could not, such as the possibility of transmitting voices through the air (ultimately leading to the invention of the radio). Tesla was sure he had received communications from intelligent creatures from other planets, and he boasted that he could split the Earth in two like an apple. He was afraid of women wearing pearl earrings, and his idea of how to behave at a dinner included calculating the cubic volume of the food on his plate.

It would be a mistake, however, to let a discussion of his odd behavior overshadow the profoundly useful and practical inventions Tesla created. It was fortunate for the world, and perhaps for Nikola Tesla as well, that George Westinghouse brought practicality to bear on Tesla's unique mind.

Tesla was born in 1856 in the small town of Smiljan, which is today located in the country of Croatia but was then part of the empire of Austria-Hungary. His father was a minister, and his mother had a reputation for being inventive. Tesla attended schools in his hometown and in the nearby city of Gospic, and he later studied at universities in Europe. In 1881 he found a job at the Central Telegraph Office in Budapest, Hungary, and while there invented a telephone amplifier (which intensifies a weak electrical current). The following year he moved to Paris, France, to work as an engineer for the Continental Edison Company, owned by Thomas Edison.

Nikola Tesla. *Reproduced by permission of the Library of Congress.*

Working for Edison

In 1884 Tesla left Europe for the United States, equipped with four cents and a job offer from Thomas Edison, who was already widely recognized as a top American inventor responsible for the spread of electricity throughout the country. But the twenty-eight-year-old immigrant from Croatia had a difference of opinion with Edison regarding the distribution of electrical currents: the subject was direct current (DC) versus alternating current (AC). Tesla explained to Edison his plans for a motor based on AC, which he found to be less problematic than DC and capable of higher voltage. Edison insisted that Tesla's designs for this new motor were impractical and dangerous.

Despite the differences of opinion, the new immigrant worked for Edison for a year, designing DC motors for the Edison Machine Works in New York City. The two inventors also had radically different approaches to their work: Edison was famous for inventing by tinkering and testing, and Tesla's approach was to imagine solutions in his head, and then to build them.

Tesla was eventually let go from Edison's labs. The differences in style were too great, and Tesla's insistence on AC threatened Edison's deeply held belief in DC.

Teaming up with Westinghouse

Almost immediately, George Westinghouse bought Tesla's patent rights to motors and transformers that used AC. Westinghouse offered Tesla a job in the Westinghouse laboratories as well as future royalties (a percentage of revenue or profits earned in the future) for the use of his ideas.

Westinghouse and his new employee launched a huge struggle with Edison over the issue of whether DC or AC would dominate. Eventually, alternating current won out, principally for two reasons: using alternating current, it was possible to send electric power over wires for many miles, whereas direct current could travel for only about two miles. Second, alternating current, unlike direct current, could be sent in a great concentration and then powered down at the far end.

Westinghouse and Edison fought bitterly over the issue of AC versus DC. Edison tried to convince government authorities that alternating current was dangerous and should be banned. (At one point, opponents of alternating current used a Westinghouse AC generator to electrocute a condemned prisoner in New York State to demonstrate its danger.) But the greater practicality of alternating current, especially the ability to distribute it over long distances from a centralized generator, became more important. AC remains the worldwide standard into the twenty-first century. The symbolic end of the struggle came in 1917, when Tesla won the highest honor awarded by the American Institute of Electric Engineers. Ironically, it is called the Edison Medal.

More original ideas

Tesla's development of alternating current was just the start of a long string of inventions. His partnership with Westinghouse gave him the opportunity to design what may have been Tesla's greatest achievement: the world's

The Basics of Electricity

What we call electricity is the flow of electrons, particles that are smaller than atoms. Flowing electrons are so small that they can squeeze between atoms and thereby flow through a length of wire. This flow of electrons is called the current, and it goes in a circle—from where it started and back again—in what is called an electric circuit.

Electrons find it easier to flow between the atoms of some materials than of others. With copper, for example, it is fairly easy for electrons to squeeze between the atoms—which is the reason that copper is most often used in electric wires.

The degree of difficulty in pushing through the atoms is called resistance. Think of trying to shove through a crowd of people. Big, heavy adults jammed into a small space would be harder to get through than a group of kids playing on a playground. When it's hard to get through the crowd of atoms, the electrons create heat (similar to the way friction creates heat when two objects are rubbed together). The more resistance there is to the flow of electrons, the more heat is generated. In fact, wires that generate a lot of resistance get so hot they glow. In a lightbulb, for example, the circuit includes a very thin wire called the filament. With a large number of

first hydroelectric generating plant. Completed in 1895 and located in Niagara Falls, New York, the plant distributed electrical current to Niagara Falls and to Buffalo, New York, some twenty-three miles away. In 1897, Westinghouse and Tesla astounded people attending the World's Fair in Chicago by using an AC generator to flip on lights throughout the fair grounds.

Tesla began working with increasing electric current that changed directions more frequently, called high-frequency. This resulted in the creation of waves that could transmit energy through the air, which is the basic principle of radio and television. He invented a device called the Tesla coil that was still used a century later in radios and other devices. (This work is the basis for the claim that it was Tesla, not the Italian inventor Guglielmo Marconi [1874–1937], who invented the radio. In 1943 the U.S. Supreme Court disallowed a key Marconi patent for radio technology, recognizing Tesla's earlier work.) Tesla also worked on the principle of the X ray at electrons trying to shove through at the same time, the filament glows brightly, which is how lightbulbs give light. When the thin filament eventually breaks (from being heated and cooled a number of times), it breaks the circuit. The bulb has "burned out." The flow of electricity can be used to create heat by increasing the resistance to the flow—the principle used in an electric toaster or oven.

There is another feature of electric current that is also highly useful. If wire is wrapped around a nail and electricity is sent through the wire (from a flashlight battery, for example), the nail becomes a magnet. Magnets can be used to push or pull things made of metal. This is the basic principle of the electric motor: a coil of wire is magnetized, and the magnetism is used to move the parts of the motor and create a rotating motion. This can be done with tiny motors, and also with huge ones (such as those used in electric train locomotives).

Unlike steam engines or engines powered with gasoline, electric motors can take electricity from wires, such as the ones inside buildings, as well as wires strung overhead along railroad tracks. An electric train, therefore, does not need to carry its own fuel—it can be sent to the train through the wires.

the same time as the German scientist Wilhelm Conrad Röntgen (1845–1923), who is generally recognized as discovering X rays. Tesla used the ability to transmit energy through the air to develop the earliest version of a remote control.

In 1899 Tesla established a research laboratory in the town of Colorado Springs, Colorado, about sixty miles south of Denver (in part, it was thought, to avoid destroying New York City with his experiments in high voltage). Using funds invested by the New York banker **J. P. Morgan** (1837–1913; see entry), Tesla worked on transmitting free energy through the air on a global scale. When Morgan heard more about Tesla's experiments, he is said to have asked: "If anyone can draw on the power, where do we put the meter?" (In other words, how can we get people to pay for this?) It was the end of Morgan's financial support.

During his stay in Colorado Springs, experimenting with wireless transmitters (that is, radio), Tesla insisted he had

A railroad signaler throws a switch on the line. Electronic railroad signals, invented by George Westinghouse, made railroads safer. *Reproduced by permission of Martha Tabor/Working Image Photographs.*

received a message from another planet or galaxy. While wireless transmission of messages on Earth could be demonstrated, interplanetary communications were difficult to believe. Along with some of his personal habits—such as showing a strong fear of germs—Tesla acquired the reputation of an extreme eccentric, even as his inventions were lighting the world.

Bringing major change to the twentieth century

George Westinghouse had licensed about forty of Tesla's patents, and he went on to build one of the great industrial empires in the United States. Royalties paid by Westinghouse helped fund Tesla's continuing experiments.

By the turn of the twentieth century, Westinghouse was said to have employed fifty thousand people in fifteen companies in the United States, Canada, and Europe. The value of his companies was about $120 million (about $6.4 billion in 2000 prices), many times the amount of Tesla's personal wealth.

Westinghouse's activities were by no means limited to the inventions of Tesla. Westinghouse was active in several areas, from building huge generators to create electricity to making home electric appliances. It was Westinghouse who built the powerful electric motors that displaced both steam and petroleum as the power for railroad locomotives, thus combining the business of making the trains move (motors) and stop (air brakes), with the signaling system that told the locomotive engineer when to do one or the other. And it was Westinghouse who developed the system used today to distribute electricity by combining the ideas of Tesla and a device based on work by Lucient Gaulard of France and John Gibbs of Britain and perfected by William Stanley (1858–1916), an American electrical engineer employed by Westinghouse.

Panic and decline

In 1907 a financial panic hit the New York Stock Exchange. Investors lost confidence in the future and started selling stocks. People also worried that their paper currency would become worthless if banks could not convert it into gold, and they started rushing to the bank to get gold while they could. The panic of 1907 marked a major transformation in the Industrial Revolution. After that point, finance emerged as even more important than engineering (designing new machines) or manufacturing. Without large sums of money, businesses could not afford to keep operating, regardless of how clever their machines or how efficient their manufacturing.

Although Westinghouse was famous for forming a new company to accommodate every new invention he made or that he licensed from others, new businesses required capital (monetary investments or loans). As a result of the financial crisis in New York, Westinghouse was suddenly expected to pay back his loans. Unable to come up with the cash, Westinghouse was forced to hand over stock, losing control of his industrial empire. By 1911 Westinghouse stopped playing an active role in the companies he had founded.

His declining business fortunes did not extinguish his inventive light, however. In 1910 he founded another company, his last, to exploit a new type of spring to take the jolts out of automobiles. The invention came to be called the shock absorber.

In his last two years of life, Westinghouse's health declined, and he was forced to use a wheelchair; he responded by working on an invention for an electric-powered version. Westinghouse died on March 12, 1914. Four years after his death a patent he had applied for was finally granted, bringing the total number of patents he received to 361.

Tesla's end

Westinghouse's business misfortunes also affected Nikola Tesla. Westinghouse could not afford to pay the generous royalties the partners had agreed upon earlier. In the meantime, Tesla had turned his attention to projects that proved far less practicable than his earlier work. He lived in a two-room hotel suite in New York City, continuing to conduct research and write magazine articles but exhibiting increasingly eccentric behavior and gradually fading into obscurity.

Tesla died in New York City in January 1943 at age eighty-six. He had few friends and little money, despite receiving hundreds of patents in his lifetime.

For More Information

Books

Aaseng, Nathan. *The Problem Solvers.* Minneapolis, MN: Lerner Publications, 1989.

Cheney, Margaret. *Tesla: Man Out of Time.* New York: Simon and Schuster, 2001.

Hunt, Inez, and Wanetta W. Draper. *Lightning in His Hand: The Life Story of Nikola Tesla.* Hawthorne, CA: Omni Publications, 1981.

Levine, I. E. *Inventive Wizard: George Westinghouse.* New York: J. Messner, 1962.

O'Neill, John J. *Prodigal Genius: The Life of Nikola Tesla.* Hollywood, CA: Angriff Press, 1981.

Seifer, Marc J. *Wizard: The Life and Times of Nikola Tesla: Biography of a Genius.* Secaucus, NJ: Carol Pub., 1996.

Thomas, Henry. *George Westinghouse.* New York: G. P. Putnam's Sons, 1960.

Periodicals

D'Alto, Nick. "Edison, Tesla, and the Battle of the Currents: Should Electricity be AC or DC?" *Odyssey,* February 2002, p. 20.

Johnson, Jeff. "'Extraordinary Science' and the Strange Legacy of Nikola Tesla." *Skeptical Inquirer,* Summer 1994, p. 366.

Johnson, Jeff. "Nikola Tesla: Genius, Visionary, and Eccentric." *Skeptical Inquirer,* Summer 1994, 368.

Johnson, Jeff. "Tesla's Inventions: A Critique." *Skeptical Inquirer,* Summer 1994, p. 372.

Leone, Marie, et al. "Edison and Tesla: The Founding Fathers of Electricity." *Electrical World,* January–February 2000, p. 41.

Usselman, Steven W. "From Novelty to Utility: George Westinghouse and the Business of Innovation during the Age of Edison." *Business History Review,* Summer 1992, p. 251.

Web Sites

"About George Westinghouse." *Library of Congress.* http://memory.loc.gov/ammem/papr/west/westgorg.html (accessed on February 18, 2003).

George Westinghouse Virtual Museum. http://www.georgewestinghouse.com/museum.html (accessed on February 18, 2003).

Kurtus, Ron. "Alternating Current Electricity (AC)." *School for Champions.* http://www.school-for-champions.com/science/ac.htm (accessed on February 18, 2003).

"Nikola Tesla." *Freedom of Information Act, Federal Bureau of Information.* http://foia.fbi.gov/tesla.htm (accessed on February 18, 2003).

"Tesla: Master of Lightning." *Public Broadcasting Service.* http://www.pbs.org/tesla/ (accessed on February 18, 2003).

Wicks, Frank. "How George Westinghouse Changed the World." *Mechanical Engineering Magazine.* http://www.memagazine.org/backissues/october96/features/westingh/westingh.html (accessed on February 18, 2003).

Eli Whitney

Born December 8, 1765
Westborough, Massachusetts

Died January 8, 1825
New Haven, Connecticut

American inventor

"He can make anything."

—Catherine Greene, recommending Eli Whitney to planters who needed a machine to comb seeds from cotton.

Reproduced by permission of the Library of Congress.

Eli Whitney is well known as the inventor of the cotton gin, a device that pulled cotton from the seed and influenced the course of American history in ways that are both obvious and subtle. The Industrial Revolution, a period of fast-paced economic change that began in Great Britain in the middle of the eighteenth century, could be said to have started influencing life in the United States in April 1793. It was in that month that Eli Whitney, a young graduate of Yale University, first demonstrated a machine for extracting the sticky, green seeds from bolls of cotton. It was a called a cotton gin (*gin* being short for *engine*).

The cotton gin had two enormous consequences for American history. First, it revived cotton as a cash crop in the South, and helped keep the South a largely agricultural economy for most of the nineteenth century. Second, cotton crops supported large plantations, where owners thought only African slaves could work during during hot, humid summer months. Slavery had been on the verge of dying out at the end of the 1700s, but cotton helped it survive and become a leading moral issue contributing to the civil war between the North and South from 1861 to 1865.

Later, Whitney's system of manufacturing identical parts enabled the efficient production of thousands of rifles, thereby contributing to the victory of the Union (that of the Northern states) in the U.S. Civil War. The system became central to the industrialization of the American economy in the second half of the nineteenth century.

Childhood and youth

Eli Whitney was born on a farm near Westborough, Massachusetts, in 1765, the oldest of four children of Eli and Elizabeth Whitney. He was born just at the time the Industrial Revolution was beginning to make an impact in England. Like all farmers in the late 1700s, Eli's father had a workshop where he used to make implements for the farm, as well as furniture for the house. There were no factories in America at the time, nor was it possible to go to stores to buy most things a farmer needed.

The life of a child in colonial America was not easy. When he was five, his mother fell ill and Eli was expected to help with chores around the house. In the winter, he tended to sixty head of cattle before walking across a mile of snow-covered fields to attend Westborough's one-room school. When he was twelve, his mother died, and Eli had to take on even more responsibility in running the household.

From an early age, Eli was proficient with his hands, working in his father's shop. He became adept at taking apart watches or clocks and repairing them for neighbors, and he learned to repair violins, or make them from scratch. (Colonists had to supply their own entertainment, and the violin, or fiddle, was often the only source of music.) He also made nails, knives, and walking canes.

Yale and beyond

At age nineteen, Whitney was eager to explore the world outside the tiny town of Westborough and was determined to attend Yale University in New Haven, Connecticut, a school for wealthy young men aiming for a career in law or the ministry. Whitney was not especially interested in these careers, but he was determined to attend Yale.

Determined to get an education, Eli Whitney entered Yale University (pictured) as a 24-year-old freshman. Upon graduation he did not follow the normal career paths of most Yale graduates of the time, instead choosing to become a teacher. *Reproduced by permission of the Corbis Corporation.*

His father did not have the money to pay the full tuition at Yale, so Whitney got a job as a schoolmaster in the nearby town of Grafton. In Whitney's day, learning to write also meant learning to make one's own pen (from a goose quill), which was one of the skills that Whitney taught. He finally entered Yale in 1789, at age twenty-four. He graduated three years later, in 1792, educated but unemployed. Since none of the career choices typically pursued by Yale graduates appealed to Whitney, he decided to return to his earlier profession, teaching.

Whitney found a job as a tutor on a plantation and traveled by packet boat (a small passenger ship that also carries freight and mail, usually along the coastline) to Savannah, Georgia. Traveling with him was another alumnus of Yale, Phineas Miller. When Whitney arrived in Savannah to take up his tutoring job, he was told that the promised pay had been cut in half. Disgusted, Whitney refused to take the job.

His traveling companion, Miller, recommended Whitney as a man of both education and mechanical ability who would be a valuable addition to the staff of his employer, Catherine Greene, the widow of Revolutionary War General Nathanael Greene (1742–1786).

Plantation shoptalk

One evening in the spring of 1793, a group of plantation owners was gathered at the Greene mansion discussing their dismal prospects. Their main crop, tobacco, had depleted the soil. The soil in Georgia was suitable for growing cotton, but only a variety of cotton that had very short fibers and sticky, green seeds in each boll. Picking the seeds from the cotton bolls was time-consuming work for a slave, an expense that hurt the profitability of growing cotton.

Catherine Greene pointed to Whitney for an answer. "He can build anything," she said, recommending that Whitney turn his attention to making a machine that could extract the seeds from cotton bolls.

Whitney set to work. In a few months he had built the first model of what he called a "cotton gin." Whitney's machine was not terribly complex. A sieve-like arrangement of wires held the cotton boll, while a rotating drum covered with hooks tugged the lint out of the boll. A brush then whisked the lint off the hooks on the drum.

Whitney's first demonstration, to a few of Catherine Greene's neighbors, was an immediate success. In one hour Whitney turned out as much seed-free cotton lint as several workers could create in a single day. He boasted that one person using a gin could do the work of ten people without one, and that if the gin were powered by water or horsepower, one worker could do the work of fifty.

With no more than a brief demonstration, the plantation owners reacted quickly. The men who saw the demonstration ordered whole fields planted with cottonseed. Word spread rapidly, and soon more cotton had been planted than Whitney could have ginned in a year.

In the meantime, Whitney returned north to obtain a patent on his machine and to plan for production, leaving his

The cotton gin made cotton farms and plantations, like this one in Arkansas, more productive and efficient. *Reproduced by permission of the Corbis Corporation.*

friend and business partner Phineas Miller behind to address the issue of raising revenue from the invention. (A patent is an exclusive right officially granted by a government to an inventor to make or sell an invention. Others who want to legally use the idea need to pay for the right to do so.)

A brilliant way of not making money

Whitney and his partner hit on a scheme to set up cotton gins and charge planters a percentage of the cotton they processed—40 percent was their proposition. Even though the cotton gin yielded large savings in the cost of removing the seeds, most planters thought Whitney's proposal was much too expensive.

As Whitney encountered delays setting up production to make a large number of gins for sale, many planters copied his idea, putting together their own versions of Whitney's patented invention and set to ginning cotton—without paying anything to Whitney and Miller. At least three hundred copies of the cotton gin had been made by 1797, even while Whitney struggled back in Connecticut to set up a factory with specialized tools to manufacture his device.

Whitney and Miller went to court repeatedly to protect Whitney's patent. But filing lawsuits was time-consuming and expensive. In the meantime, more and more illegal copies of the gin were produced, supporting a dramatic rise in cotton production throughout the South. Although Whitney and Miller succeeded in some suits, the monetary awards were often less than the cost of filing the suit in the first place.

The two inventors tried another approach in 1801, licensing the gin to entire states which could then authorize planters to legally copy the design. This approach eventually earned the partners about $90,000, which was a large sum in the early nineteenth century—but not enough to make either man wealthy.

As a financial proposition for Whitney, the cotton gin was a failure. The costs he incurred in pursuing lawsuits for patent infringement, and for setting up a factory in New Haven, ate away most of the money he ever saw for his invention.

King cotton

For the United States, and for the South in particular, the cotton gin had an enormous impact. Cotton was easy to grow, and with the cotton gin, it was relatively easy to process.

The rapid expansion of cotton fields raised a need for more farm workers, and in the South this meant slaves. Although the United States banned the import of slaves from 1808 onward, their numbers nevertheless grew, and slavery came to be viewed as an essential ingredient to the economy of the South.

The flood of inexpensive cotton in the United States made possible by Whitney's invention resulted in a revolution in fabrics. American cotton was shipped to newly automated textile factories in both England and New England, where another development of the Industrial Revolution—

automated spinning and weaving machines—was resulting in huge changes in the way cloth was manufactured. Cotton shoved its way ahead of wool, flax (linen), and silk to become the leading raw material of cloth.

Muskets to the rescue

For Whitney, the cotton gin had been the source of ruination rather than success. He was thirty-nine years old and had nothing to show for the past decade except a record of unsuccessful lawsuits. In 1804 he turned his back on the cotton gin and on the South. He returned to New Haven in search of a new project.

But, as would happen often during the Industrial Revolution, the government came to the inventor's rescue. In the 1790s many people thought that there was a risk of war, either with England or with France (those two countries were at war with one another almost constantly after the French Revolution in 1789). The United States, which remained neutral, continued to trade with both countries, which made some political leaders feel that they might be attacked. This, in turn, created a desire to improve the preparedness of the army, and this meant acquiring many more muskets (an early form of rifle).

Two men are depicted working on a cotton gin at a marketplace. Eli Whitney's invention sparked an agricultural revolution in the South, and cotton became a cash crop. *Reproduced by permission of the Library of Congress.*

Up to that time, the federal government had been making its own muskets in two armories, one located in Springfield, Massachusetts, not far from Whitney's birthplace, the other at Harper's Ferry, Virginia (now in West Virginia). The muskets of the time were handcrafted by skilled workers and as such took a long time to make. Moreover, each musket was unique; if one broke, or a part failed, there were no replacement parts on hand for a quick fix.

Whitney, desperate to find some other project to keep the workers in his New Haven factory busy, offered to produce muskets for the federal government. On June 14, 1798, he signed a contract to manufacture ten thousand muskets over twenty-eight months for a total price of $134,000. And so began the second phase of Whitney's remarkable career.

Creating the parts to make the whole

Today, Whitney's idea for mass production techniques and the interchangeability of manufacturing parts seems obvious because it is now common practice. Specifically, Whitney resolved to make identical parts of muskets, which could be assembled into what would be ten thousand identical muskets. Extra parts could be made to replace any that broke or failed.

To succeed, the parts of a musket needed to fit together exactly, which meant that each part needed to be truly identical to the others. Most metal and wood work at the time was done by individual skilled workers. While handmade musket stocks (the wooden part that fits against the shoulder) and barrels (the long metal tube through which the bullet flies) might be very similar, such parts were, by nature, not exactly identical. This was the challenge faced by Whitney.

Making the tools to make the tools

Another aspect of Whitney's challenge was the lack of skilled workers at the time. He instead devised a system of manufacturing that would employ unskilled laborers using "machine tools," tools devised to manufacture machines.

An easy way to envision Whitney's system is to think of a pattern for a dress. A pattern is put up against the material, and scissors are guided exactly around the edge of the pattern. No matter how many times this is done, the material that is cut out will be the same shape as every other piece of material cut out from the same pattern.

The process of making a musket from wood and iron parts was a bit more complex, partly because it is harder to cut and shape wood and iron than it is to cut out fabric. Whitney spent months designing and making a series of patterns, or templates, and devices that could automate the process. The tools designed by Whitney had to be relatively easy to operate by unskilled workers.

Whitney soon fell behind the established schedule. After two years, he still had not delivered any muskets. He applied for, and received, one extension after another. In the end, it took him almost eight years to fill the entire order of ten thousand guns. But shortly thereafter, in 1811, Whitney got another contract to produce fifteen thousand more muskets, which he manufactured within just two years, thereby proving the success of his system. The War of 1812 assured Whitney's success by yielding yet more contracts.

Whitney did not invent the idea of using interchangeable or standardized parts. Other people in the United States and the world were hard at work inventing labor-saving technology. However, Whitney was one of the first to carry out and perfect what came to be called "the interchangeable system" of manufacturing. This important contribution puts him at the forefront of the growth of American industry.

Getting personal

For a quarter of a century, Whitney had devoted himself to his business. Although he had friends and family, he spent the majority of his time working and thus had little time for a personal life. Finally, in 1817, at the age of fifty-one, Whitney married Henrietta Edwards. Three years later, Whitney's only son, also named Eli, was born. Over the next eight years, the couple would have four children, the youngest of which died while still a baby.

After 1820, when Whitney began to suffer from poor health, his nephews were left to operate his factory until his son, Eli Whitney III, was old enough to assume responsibility. Whitney died in New Haven, Connecticut, on January 8, 1825.

For More Information

Books

Green, Constance McLaughlin. *Eli Whitney and the Birth of American Technology.* Boston, MA: Little, Brown, 1956.

Hays, Wilma Pitchford. *Eli Whitney, Founder of Modern Industry.* New York: F. Watts, 1965.

Latham, Jean Lee. *The Story of Eli Whitney.* New York: Harper and Row, 1962.

Wilson, Mitchell. *American Science and Invention: A Pictorial History.* New York: Simon and Schuster, 1954.

Periodicals

Baida, Peter. "Eli Whitney's Other Talent." *American Heritage,* May–June 1987, p. 22.

Paul, Mark. "When Cotton Became King." *Senior Scholastic,* November 13, 1981, p. 18.

Web Sites

"Eli Whitney." *Invention Dimension, Massachusetts Institute of Technology.* http://web.mit.edu/invent/iow/whitney.html (accessed on February 20, 2003).

Eli Whitney Museum. http://www.eliwhitney.org/ew.htm (accessed on February 20, 2003).

Index

References to photos are marked by (ill.); **boldface** indicates main entries and their page numbers.

A

B

C

D

E

F

G

H

I

J

K

L

M

N

O

P

Q

R

S

T

U

V

W

X

Y